Popular Mechanics

REMODELING FOR EASY ACCESS LIVING

R I C K   P E T E R S

HEARST BOOKS
A Division of Sterling Publishing Co., Inc.
New York

Copyright © 2006 by Rick Peters

All rights reserved. The written instructions and photographs in this volume are intended for the personal use of the reader and may be reproduced for that purpose only. Any other use, especially commercial use, is forbidden under law without the written permission of the copyright holder.

Every effort has been made to ensure that all the information in this book is accurate. However, due to differing conditions, tools, and individual skills, the publisher cannot be responsible for any injuries, losses, and/or other damages that may result from the use of the information in this book.

Note: The safety guards were removed for clarity in many of the photographs in this book. Make sure to always use all safety devices according to the manufacturers' instructions.

Remodeling for Easy Access Living production staff:
Design: Sandy Freeman
Cover design: Celia Fuller
Contributing writer: Cheryl A. Romano
Photography: Christopher J. Vendetta
Cover photo: Timberlake Cabinet Company (www.timberlake.com)
Illustrations: Triad Design Group
Copy editor: Barbara McIntosh Webb
Page layout: Triad Design Group
Index: Nan Badgett

Safety Note: Homes built prior to 1978 may have been constructed with hazardous materials: lead and asbestos. You can test painted surfaces with a test kit available at most hardware stores. Asbestos can be found in ceiling and wall materials, joint compound, insulation, and flooring. Hire a professional licensed hazardous-removal company to check for this, and remove any if hazardous materials are found.

Library of Congress Cataloging-in-Publication Data available.

10 9 8 7 6 5 4 3 2 1

Published by Hearst Books
A Division of Sterling Publishing Co., Inc.
387 Park Avenue South, New York, NY 10016

Popular Mechanics and Hearst Books are trademarks of Hearst Communications, Inc.

www.popularmechanics.com

Distributed in Canada by Sterling Publishing
c/o Canadian Manda Group, 165 Dufferin Street
Toronto, Ontario, Canada M6K 3H6

Distributed in Australia by Capricorn Link (Australia) Pty. Ltd.
P.O. Box 704, Windsor, NSW 2756 Australia

Manufactured in China

ISBN-13: 978-1-58816-465-0

ISBN-10: 1-58816-465-9

Foreword by Mary Jo Peterson, CKD, CBD, CAPS

At a time when the age boom is impacting on all aspects of our culture, this book offers inspiration and information to help each of us improve our home and the quality of life for all who enter it. In the life of a home, natural changes occur as both the home and its owners age. Smart planning will incorporate renovations that support the active aging we are all hoping to experience. A number of these concepts, sometimes referred to as universal design or design for aging in place, are illustrated throughout *Remodeling for Easy Access Living*, showing us ideas that will improve the value of any home by making it more livable for a greater variety of people.

The first book of its kind, *Remodeling for Easy Access Living* is more than a discussion of what can be done, as it takes an existing home and demonstrates how age-appropriate changes can be executed. In this book, complete with before and after plans and images, Rick Peters has taken a moderately priced ranch-style home and detailed changes that are realistic, affordable, and attractive. Design for aging in place is not "all or nothing," as each effort improves the usability and safety of a home. This home includes many of these changes—providing lever handles and wider hallways, having easy-to-use controls on lighting and appliance and locating them within safe reach of most people, and more.

It does so in a way that takes good user-friendly design from intellectual concept to reality, making *Remodeling for Easy Access Living* a must-have for the bookshelf of any one of us who is living the age boom and wants it to be a positive experience.

Acknowledgments

For all their help, advice, and support, I offer special thanks to:

Connie Edwards, CKD, CKB, Director of Design at Timberlake Cabinet Company, for designing the beautifully accessible kitchen, and for supplying the fine cabinets to create it.

Mary Jo Peterson, CKD, CBD, CAPS, America's foremost expert on Universal Design, for her insights in shaping the makeover projects.

Nora DePalma of Building Profits, Inc., for the perfect American Standard fixtures and faucets used in both bathrooms, and for the DPI AquaTile wallboard in the guest bath.

Shelby Heimbach of Purdie Rogers, for the stunning Staron by Samsung countertop gracing the kitchen, and for the sleek, low-threshold shower and door by Lasco Bathware used in the master bath (thanks, too, to Shelly Roberts at Lasco).

Tom Fitzgerald of BathEase, for the award-winning, walk-in bathtub featured in the guest bath makeover.

Matt Spaulding of Spaulding Communications and LaShon McGinnis from Honeywell Nylon, for the lush, mature-friendly carpet of Anso nylon from Blueridge Home.

Bob Srenaski of Safe-Access Systems, Inc., for the practical and attractive safety bars and accessories used in the guest bath makeover.

Rob Jenkins of Rev-A-Shelf, for the pull-out and pull-down shelving that made the kitchen and laundry room extra-accessible.

Craig Weaver of ODL, for the glass pocket door inserts that led beautifully from the kitchen to the laundry room.

Michael Rabinovitz of Ingersoll-Rand, for the easy-to-use, gleaming Schlage lever handsets and deadbolt.

Todd Makela and crew at The Top Shop, Prescott, AZ, for a great job installing the Staron countertop.

Terri Brahm of Terri's Floors, Prescott Valley, AZ, for the quality carpet padding used with the Honeywell Anso nylon carpet.

The folks at Hunter Fan, for the low-profile, remote-controlled ceiling fans for saving energy costs in the living room/dining areas.

Miele USA, for the ultra-maneuverable, state-of-the-art vacuum cleaner with HEPA filter.

Heather Leary of Verilux, the Healthy Lighting Company, for the high-tech HappyEyes lamps illuminating the living area.

Brian Maynard of KitchenAid Home Appliances, for helping provide all the high-access, high-appeal appliances used in the kitchen.

Christopher Vendetta, for taking great photographs under unusually demanding conditions.

Rob Lembo and the crew at Triad Design Group, for illustrations and page layouts.

Barb Webb, copyediting whiz, for ferreting out mistakes and gently suggesting corrections.

Heartfelt thanks to my constant inspiration: Cheryl, Lynne, Will, and Beth.

Contents

Introduction

Are you 50, 60, 70+, or have a loved one who is? Do you or a loved one need help to move around, see, or hear? Then you may already know why this is such a valuable book. You've heard about the aging of America...accessible design...aging in place...and you know that if it hasn't all touched your life yet, it will—and maybe soon.

This book isn't just about the changes that make a home more comfortable and safe as we age or deal with a physical challenge—there are many such books already. *Remodeling for Easy Access Living* shows the how-to that's behind the changes, so you can do the work yourself or hire it out with confidence.

Here we don't throw a fantasy budget at a mansion and show off the pretty results. We've taken a real, very modest home and transformed almost every room to be more open, more con-

venient, more accessible to all—with affordable products available to almost everyone.

You'll find the makeover material divided into three sections. "Planning Your Makeover" covers the fundamentals of accessible home styles, expert design guidelines, product trends, and more. In "Real Makeover Examples," you'll see the real-life home makeovers, complete with before-and-after photos and costs. Finally, in "Creating Your New Look," you'll go step-by-step through the basics that let you achieve your own results.

Here's to your makeover success for your accessible home.

—James Meigs
Editor-in-Chief, *Popular Mechanics*

Planning Your Makeover

The stairs are too steep, the floor's too slippery. The freezer's out of reach, the bathtub is dangerous. In some important way or ways, your house isn't keeping up with your needs, and you know that changes need to be made. The question is, what changes? And in which rooms? In this section, we'll help you plan the updates you need to adapt your place to your life now. You'll read about basics in accessibility, safety, and convenience, and the suitable products and materials available today.

Here you'll find step-by-step looks at the basics you need to know in the most important areas: room design, choosing materials, and systems (electrical, plumbing, and framing). If you want (and can do) a wholesale makeover yourself, you'll find out how, from installing a low-threshold shower to upgrading windows. Just want the basics on easy-access appliances, or upgrading to paddle-style light switches? You'll find those here, too.

Ready for updates to make your home more accessible, more mature-friendly? Sounds like a plan.

ACCESSIBLE DESIGN

As we age, our homes often don't keep up with us. Door handles are trickier to open...the bathtub is tougher to get in and out of...the oven is too low...our lamps are too dim. For millions of Americans and their families, these "growing pains" are more than just inconvenient: They can reduce safety and standards of living, and eventually these issues can accumulate to force a move out of a cherished home.

Happily, though, there are lots of ways to make a home more accessible and mature-friendly. Today's products, materials, and focus on the needs of the senior market offer options that just weren't available to previous generations. Whether a home needs a little or a lot of work to keep up with a mature lifestyle, here you'll find ideas to increase comfort, safety, and convenience—for people of all ages and abilities. In this chapter, we'll look at some of the physical changes that come with age, and how you can modify your home to help it adapt to your changing needs.

Aging in Place

■ "Home" is a powerful idea. It's where we feel safe, in control, and independent. It's where we decide what to eat, when to sleep, making all the choices that make up a self-determined life. No wonder, then, that more than 83% of homeowners over age 50 want to stay in their current homes for the rest of their lives, according to the AARP (American Association of Retired Persons).

Time, though, can have different ideas. Age may bring wisdom, but it often brings along a host of physical changes that can make a home out-dated. This is especially true when you consider that most "standard" dimensions in housing go back several decades. Things as basic as the width of a door or the height of a counter were determined primarily for U.S. veterans returning from World War II. So, if you're tall, strong, and young, the standard home specs should suit you.

In one way or another, many of us don't fit a standard. That's why the concept of "universal design" is gaining strength: It's an approach to homes, products, and public buildings that accommodates people of all ages and all abilities. (This book doesn't focus exclusively on universal design, but reflects many elements of this important movement.) As Mary Jo Peterson, the acknowledged "queen" of universal design, says in the foreword to this book, "Design for aging in place is not 'all or nothing,' as each effort improves the usability and safety of a home." The key word is "accessible," whether we're talking about a bathroom or a laundry room shelf, a hallway or a set of oven controls.

Physical changes, home changes. For most of us, the goal is to stay in our homes safely, comfortably, and independently. Experts call this "aging in place". Here is a glimpse of some of the common physical changes that age brings (sourced from the respected Mayo Clinic), followed by examples of their impact on aging in place:

■ **Vision.** Starting in one's 40s, close-up focus starts to blur. Vision loss can stem from diseases like glaucoma and macular degeneration. It can become more difficult to read a warning on a cleaning product; misjudging a counter edge may result in glass breakage and injury.

■ **Joints/bones/muscles.** After age 35, bones lose size and density. Muscles and joints slowly lose some strength and flexibility with age. (Ailments like arthritis and osteoporosis also reduce flexibility and strength.) Reaching for and grasping everyday items, turning switches on and off, navigating across a thick carpet can all become challenges.

■ **Body temperature.** A decrease in perspiration may make it tougher to stay comfortable when temperatures rise. Trying to stay cool could cost more in energy use for air conditioners and floor fans.

■ **Hearing.** One in every three people over age 60 has "significant" hearing loss. Inability to hear a doorbell or unexpected noise can increase worry over security.

Now see how these physical changes can be accommodated by modifying the home:

■ **Vision.** Upgrade lighting over workspaces and reading places. Use color contrasts to help differentiate elements, such as light-hued kitchen cabinets with a boldly colored and edged countertop.

■ **Joints/bones/muscles.** Install easy-to-use paddle switches for light control; buy an extender/reach tool for items in tall cabinets; replace thick carpet with low-profile, tight-weave versions; add grab bars in bathrooms; replace a freestanding kitchen range with a wall oven and cooktop.

■ **Body temperature.** Increase comfort and lower energy costs with ceiling fans (remote controls make this even easier).

■ **Hearing.** Buy an amplifying device for doorbells; consider one of the more affordable new video security systems.

Of course, this partial list doesn't include the devices that are part of everyday life for many people, such as walkers and wheelchairs. These can require larger-scale changes, such as widening a hallway, expanding a bathroom entry, and replacing flooring. But these are still doable modifications that can help keep a home truly livable for a longer period of time.

KITCHENS

Although it's probably not obvious, all of the sleek, appealing kitchens shown on this page are suitable for aging in place. And that's what's great about them—they're all accessible and attractive. There are a number of traits that all well-designed, accessible kitchens share: walkway clearances, efficient work triangles, multi-level countertops, easy-to-use hardware, and good lighting.

Walkway clearance. A fully accessible kitchen has walkways that are wide and clear, as shown in the top photo. This allows for smooth travel in any mode: walking, walking with a cane, using a walker, or in a wheelchair. You'll notice there are no throw rugs on the floor—these are extreme tripping hazards and should be avoided. For more on recommended kitchen clearances, see pages 14–15.

Efficient work triangle. Although gigantic kitchens with wide-open spaces may be attractive to many, they're not very efficient for the cook. The work triangle—that is, the path defined by connecting the work areas (the sink, cooktop, and refrigerator)—should be fairly small to prevent unneeded walking. Notice the tight triangle in the kitchen in the middle photo. This kind of compact design not only saves steps, but it's also attractive. For more on the work triangle and recommended distances, see pages 13 and 14, respectively.

Multi-height countertops. Countertops with multiple heights offer work surfaces at varying levels to accommodate cooks and helpers of all sizes, whether seated or standing. The kitchen shown in the bottom photo offers multiple-height counters and also provides pull-up wheelchair access at the end counter.

Hardware. Hardware in the fully accessible kitchen, whether mounted to a cabinet or on an appliance, should be easy to use without having to grip it with your fingers. This generally calls for large pulls and not knobs. The hand should be able to slip into the pull and open the door without having to wrap fingers around the hardware. Pulls work best for little hands, too.

Lighting. Finally, all accessible kitchens should be well lighted. Work surfaces—especially countertops—should be lighted with overhead lights or under-cabinet lights. It's a fact that as we age, our eyes need more light; this can be accomplished by adding under-cabinet lighting (page 177) or recessed lighting (pages 178–179).

KITCHEN LAYOUTS

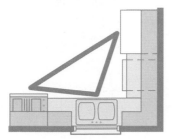

Corridor Kitchen

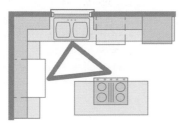

L-Shaped Kitchen

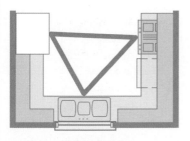

L-Shaped Kitchen with Island

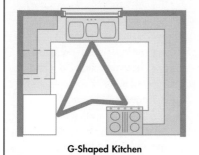

U-Shaped Kitchen

G-Shaped Kitchen

■ The existing layout or design of your kitchen will have a large impact on what you can do with it to make it more accessible and mature-friendly. If you find the current design too limiting, consider hiring a kitchen design pro to offer suggestions. Often a much more efficient and usable space can be created by removing a wall or a portion of a wall. For more on working with pros, see page 29. Most kitchens are designed using one of the following five layouts and associated work triangles, as illustrated in the drawing at left.

Corridor kitchen. For a single cook, a corridor kitchen can be quite efficient, as long as the work centers are grouped close together. The big disadvantage of this plan is that household traffic usually must flow through the space as well.

L-shaped kitchen.
Generous counter space is the biggest advantage of an L-shaped plan. Care must be taken to group the work centers together; otherwise, you have an elongated work triangle that creates wasted steps.

L-shaped with island. By adding a freestanding island to an L-shaped kitchen, you can tighten up the work triangle as well as increase storage space. An extended countertop on the island can also provide seating for an eating area. Be aware that adding an island to an existing kitchen can create narrow walkways and should be designed carefully to prevent this.

U-shaped. Considered by many the most efficient of all kitchen plans, the U-shaped configuration saves steps by closely grouping the work centers. The cook is also surrounded by plenty of countertop and storage space.

G-shaped. A derivative of the U-shape, the G-shaped plan adds an extra wall of cabinets and countertop that wrap around to become a peninsula—often this peninsula is used as an eating area. The only disadvantage to this layout is that it can give the kitchen an enclosed feeling.

KITCHEN GUIDELINES

It's sad that many kitchens are designed without giving thought to the cook. Sure, an expansive, glitzy kitchen might be gorgeous to look at, but will a cook truly enjoy working in the space? And will it be safe and mature-friendly? One of the biggest factors that affects how enjoyable—and accessible—a kitchen is to work in is work flow. Work flow is how a meal flows from start to finish, from pulling the ingredients out of the refrigerator and pantry to setting the table. In years past, only three areas were considered: the refrigerator, the sink, and the range. These three constitute the work triangle that is still used in kitchen design today, as illustrated in the drawing below left.

Work triangle. The NKBA (National Kitchen and Bath Association) recommends that no single side of the triangle be more than 9 feet, and that the combined length of the sides not exceed 26 feet. But in today's kitchens the triangle is more like a polygon: cooktop, sink, refrigerator, wall oven, microwave...you get the idea. The best way to see if a kitchen layout will work for you is to mentally "rehearse" cooking a meal or two in it. Think about your steps, from start to finish. Odds are you'll find that you keep bumping into something, or that you have to walk around an island or peninsula too much. Alter the design as necessary to remedy such faults.

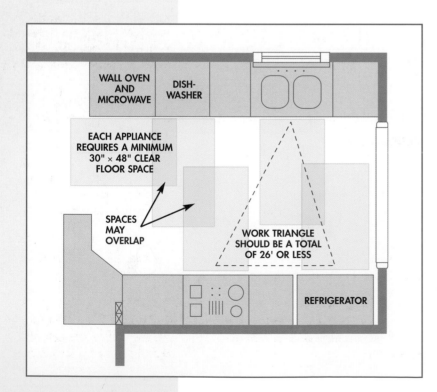

WALL OVEN AND MICROWAVE

DISH-WASHER

EACH APPLIANCE REQUIRES A MINIMUM 30" × 48" CLEAR FLOOR SPACE

SPACES MAY OVERLAP

WORK TRIANGLE SHOULD BE A TOTAL OF 26' OR LESS

REFRIGERATOR

Appliance floor space. In addition to work flow, it's important to note that each appliance in a kitchen requires a minimum of clear floor space to ensure full accessibility, as illustrated in the drawing at left. These spaces ensure that cooks in wheelchairs can fully access each appliance. For additional ways to enhance appliance access, see pages 15 and 97.

STANDARD CLEARANCES FOR WALKWAYS

FRIDGE

42"–48" MINIMUM

WALL OVEN

36" MINIMUM   32" MINIMUM

Recommended clearances. One guideline to pay particular attention to in an accessible kitchen is the recommended clearances between cabinets, islands, and walls, as illustrated in the top drawing.

Not only do these clearances provide sufficient space for two people to pass each other, but they also allow for wheelchair access. In addition to creating access, wider walkways look good and can make even a small kitchen look big, as shown in the top left photo.

Although the NKBA lists over 40 guidelines for a kitchen, we've condensed these into some general rules as follows:

1) Make sure there's at least 3 feet of countertop space in the mixing/food preparation area.
2) The counter should be at least 9" wide on one side and at least 15" on the other side of a cooktop.
3) For the sink, the counter should be at least 18" wide on one side and at least 24" on the other side.
4) Create a staging area for the oven—a spot where you can place a roast or casserole while you open or close the door—a 15"-wide counter on one side of a built-in oven or on an island that's no more than 48" from the oven.
5) A refrigerator should also have a 15"-wide counter space that's no more than 48" from the refrigerator.
6) The dishwasher should be within 36" of the sink.
7) Leave at least 21" between the dishwasher and nearby appliances or counters to allow for loading and unloading.
8) Plan at least 12" to 19" of legroom under eating areas in islands, peninsulas, etc.
9) Create as much accessible storage space as possible.
10) Provide plenty of overall lighting and don't forget task lighting at the sink, range, and food preparation areas.

KITCHEN GUIDELINES

SINK

ROLL-OUT CART CREATES KNEE SPACE NEXT TO WALL OVEN

WALL OVEN

45" 36" 25"

Raised appliances, Another way to make a kitchen more accessible is to raise up some of the appliances. Many appliances, including the dishwasher and range, can be made much more accessible by raising them 9" to 12" above the floor. A raised appliance reduces the need to bend over and exert yourself, whether you're standing, or sitting in a wheelchair. Any appliance can be raised, including the washer and dryer shown in the laundry room in the bottom left photo. For more on raising appliances, see page 96.

BATHROOMS

■ Of all the rooms in the home, the bathroom requires the most physical exertion, from getting in and out of a tub or shower to using a toilet. A mature-friendly bathroom acknowledges that as we get older we lose some mobility and strength. This doesn't mean, though, that an accessible bathroom has to look institutional. On the contrary, with some sound design and aging-friendly products, you can make over a bathroom so it's fully usable and good-looking, too. So what makes a bathroom mature-friendly? Much has to do with the fixtures and their placement. Also, the addition of grab bars (pages 46 and 164–165) can make using any fixture easier.

Sinks and faucets. To provide maximum access to those seated or standing, bathroom sinks should be wall-mounted, as shown in the top right photo. Wall-mounting a sink allows wheelchair access and creates plenty of toe room even when using a walker. The handles of the sink faucet should be levers and not knobs so they're easy to operate. For more on lever-style faucets and wall-mounted sinks, see pages 154–155 and 156–159, respectively.

Toilets. There are new breeds of toilets available that are easier to use for everyone. Most fixture makers now offer toilets with higher seats to make sitting down and getting up easier. Another option for toilets is to go with a wall-hung or in-wall toilet, as shown in the middle photo. These create better access by reducing how far the toilet extends out into the room. In small baths, an in-wall toilet can make the difference between the bathroom being wheelchair-accessible and not. For more on toilet types, see page 47.

Tubs and showers. Getting in and out of a tub or shower can be a real challenge as we age. Fixture makers now offer tubs and showers that are mature-friendly. Lasco (lascobathware.com) offers shower units with low thresholds that can also be recessed into the floor so a wheelchair can roll right in. If you like to soak in a tub but don't like the idea of stepping over the rim, BathEase (www.bathease.com) makes a tub with a door that allows you to walk right in; for more on tubs and showers, see page 45.

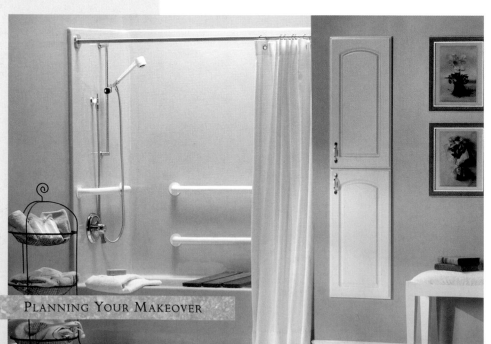

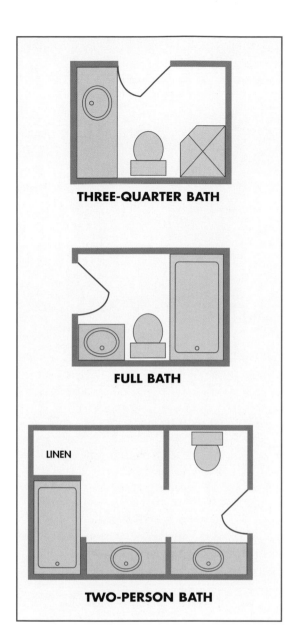

THREE-QUARTER BATH

FULL BATH

LINEN

TWO-PERSON BATH

BATHROOM LAYOUTS

Whether the bathroom you're making over is small or large, the best layout is the one that works best for you. While that may sound oversimplified, it isn't: There is no magic formula for placing a toilet, sink, bath, and other elements to create your upgraded bathroom. As long as a bathroom works for your needs, your taste, your budget, and the size of the space, it works. Most bathrooms use one of the three layouts described below and illustrated in the left drawing: three-quarter bath, full bath, and two-person bath.

Three-quarter bath. The three-quarter bath is typically a second bath in a home. The larger full bath is usually reserved for the master bedroom, but may also serve as the guest bath. All that's missing in the three-quarter bath is a tub. Because space is limited, these small bathrooms can be a real challenge to make mature-friendly—particularly if you want the bathroom to be wheelchair-accessible. In many cases a design pro (page 29) can offer suggestions for enlarging the space to provide full access. Replacing a standard door with a pocket door (see pages 140–142) can often free up needed space.

Full bath. A full bath is also called a family bath since it's sometimes used by everyone in the family. A 5' × 7' space is the minimum to allow for toilet, sink, and tub/shower. With just a bit more space, you can compartmentalize the toilet and tub for privacy, and keep the sink area open for grooming. By downsizing a full bath to a three-quarter bath you may be able to create enough space for wheelchair access (see pages 18–19 for recommended clearances).

Two-person bath. A two-person bath by its very nature is generally larger than a full bath. The identifying features of a two-person bathroom are a double sink and often a separate toilet area. This creates "usage zones" so two people can use the bathroom at the same time. Often just adding a partition wall will permit a measure of toilet privacy, leaving the sink and tub free for another's use. Here again, clearances are important; see pages 18–19.

BATHROOM GUIDELINES

Just as they do for the kitchen, the folks at the NKBA (National Kitchen and Bath Association) offer general bathroom design guidelines. Most of these guidelines can be grouped into two categories: recommended clearances and general guidelines.

Recommended clearances. Bathroom clearance recommendations are as follows and are illustrated in the drawing at right.
1) Doorways should be at least 32" wide.
2) Allow for clear floor space at least as wide as the door on the push side, and a larger clear space on the opposite side.
3) At the sink, try for clear floor space at least 30" × 48", parallel or perpendicular to the sink.
4) Plan a minimum of 48" clear floor space in front of a toilet.
5) At a tub, the recommended clear floor space is 60" × 30" for a parallel approach, or 60" × 48" for a perpendicular approach.
6) The clear floor spaces at each fixture may overlap.
7) The suggested turning radius for the bath overall is 60".
8) The minimum clearance from the centerline of a sink to any side wall is 15".
9) The minimum clearance between two sinks is 30".
10) An enclosed shower should be at least 34" × 34"; in tight quarters, 32" × 32".
11) The minimum clearance from the centerline of a toilet or bidet to any obstruction is 16".
12) The minimum compartmental toilet area is 36" × 66", with a swing-out or pocket door.

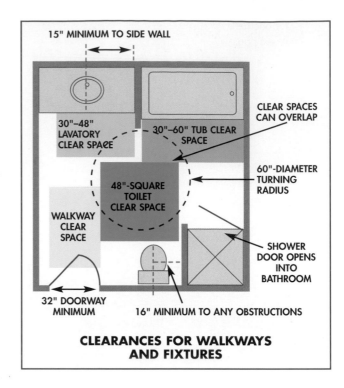

CLEARANCES FOR WALKWAYS AND FIXTURES

15" MINIMUM TO SIDE WALL
30"–48" LAVATORY CLEAR SPACE
30"–60" TUB CLEAR SPACE
CLEAR SPACES CAN OVERLAP
48"-SQUARE TOILET CLEAR SPACE
60"-DIAMETER TURNING RADIUS
WALKWAY CLEAR SPACE
SHOWER DOOR OPENS INTO BATHROOM
32" DOORWAY MINIMUM
16" MINIMUM TO ANY OBSTRUCTIONS

General guidelines.
1) Flooring should be slip-resistant.
2) All electrical receptacles, lights, and switches should have GFCIs (ground-fault circuit interrupters).
3) Both overhead and side lighting are recommended for the vanity area.
4) Open edges on countertops should be rounded or mitered.
5) All glass used should be safety-rated: laminated glass with a plastic inner layer, tempered glass, or approved plastics.

SHOWERS, TUBS, AND GRAB BARS

Since showers and tubs offer some of the greatest physical challenges in the accessible bathroom, there are specific guidelines for placing and equipping them:
1) Shower doors should open into the room.
2) Grab bars should be placed within easy reach of tub and/or shower, as illustrated in the drawing at right.
3) The shower and/or tub area should be well lighted.
4) Showers should include seating.
5) Whenever possible, the standard showerhead should be replaced with a handheld shower spray that can be adjusted to varying heights.

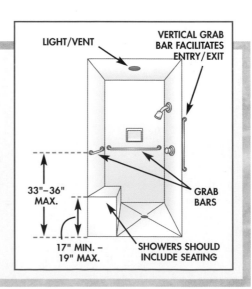

LIGHT/VENT
VERTICAL GRAB BAR FACILITATES ENTRY/EXIT
GRAB BARS
33"–36" MAX.
17" MIN. – 19" MAX.
SHOWERS SHOULD INCLUDE SEATING

Most accessible or mature-friendly bathroom makeovers will require replacing or upgrading a fixture or fixtures. This may also be the ideal time to add another sink or expand into wasted hallway space for a private toilet compartment.

If you've got a new layout in mind for your makeover—that is, you plan to move fixtures—it's important to understand how your current bathroom is plumbed in relation to what plumbing you'll need for the new layout. (For more on plumbing systems, see page 55.)

The amount of work and cost involved with the new layout will depend on how many walls currently have plumbing and how many walls in the new bathroom will need new plumbing. There are three common plumbing layouts: one-wall, two-wall, and three-wall, as illustrated in the drawing at right. Each describes how many walls are plumbed. Generally, the least expensive way to go is to use the same plumbing layout you currently have.

One-wall plumbing. The most common and simplest of all plumbing layouts is the one-wall system. Here, all the plumbing for the entire bathroom is consolidated in a single wall, as shown in the top photo. One-wall layouts are often the only feasible choice for small bathrooms.

Two-wall plumbing. When plumbing lines are extended to an adjoining wall, it allows for more flexibility, even in small bathrooms, as shown in the bottom photo. This type of layout requires additional cutting into the framing and will definitely use more piping. Often you can generate additional space around the sink with this layout.

Three-wall plumbing. With the growing popularity of separate spa showers, toilet compartments, and specialty tubs, three-wall plumbing is becoming more common. This type of layout requires the most cutting into framing and piping, and can be quite expensive to have done professionally. Because of this, design professionals generally try to keep the plumbing to two walls.

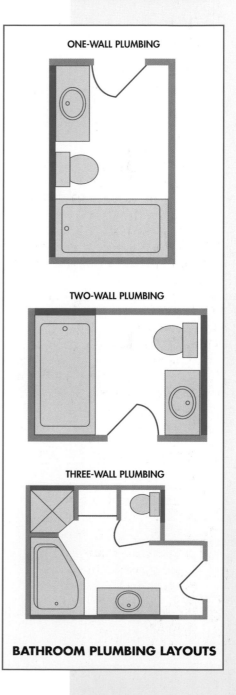

ONE-WALL PLUMBING

TWO-WALL PLUMBING

THREE-WALL PLUMBING

BATHROOM PLUMBING LAYOUTS

LIVING SPACES

■ Although every room in your home is living space, we use the term to focus on living rooms, dining rooms, and bedrooms—basically, the non-kitchen, non-bath areas that you can improve. And that's the good news for these makeovers: Because complex plumbing and electrical systems are not involved, the costs can be minimal—and ditto for the skills needed to do the projects. Because these are simple rooms, making them accessible is a matter of paying attention to details. These details can include lighting, flooring, and minimizing obstacles.

Lighting. Good lighting is important in every room in the house. Sufficient light makes everyday tasks easier and helps prevent accidents like tripping on a misplaced object on the floor, because you can see better. Large windows like the one shown in the top left photo provide plenty of natural light during the day. Overhead and accent lighting, such as table, desk, and floor lamps, light the way at night. Note that all wall switches should be converted to paddle-style switches since these are much easier to operate for people of all ages. For more on paddle-style switches, see page 176.

Minimizing obstacles. Living spaces should be laid out and furnished with minimum clutter. Minimizing obstacles, especially on the floor, is one of the best ways to prevent tripping. Lack of clutter also facilitates cleaning, while making it easier to find things, too.

Flooring. Proper flooring—as well as the transitions between flooring, such as carpet to tile—can make a huge difference in the accessibility of your room. Bathrooms, kitchens, entryways, etc., are best covered with non-slip ceramic or vinyl tile. Living spaces can be covered with either of these; but for living and bedrooms, most prefer a low-pile carpet that's softer on the feet. Transitions should be level (or ramped if absolutely necessary) to avoid tripping hazards. For more on flooring choices and transitions, see page 36.

LIVING SPACE LAYOUTS

■ What makes a living space mature-friendly? A design that offers easy access and no or limited hallways.

Easy access. Access—particularly for those in a wheelchair—is a huge issue in the design of living spaces. For a home to be fully accessible, it must be barrier-free—that is, offer no barriers to people of any age or ability. Common barriers include steps or stairs, protruding thresholds at doorways, stepped transitions where flooring changes, doors and hallways that aren't sufficiently wide, and lack of turning radii in rooms, entryways, and hallways. Even something as simple as a door or a window can be a barrier if it's hard to operate. A good example of easy access is illustrated in the left drawing below. Notice that ramps are placed at both entry points of the home. The floor plan is fairly wide open, and the master bath offers a pocket door and a curb-less or barrier-free shower. The dining and living spaces are adjacent with no wall separating them, to eliminate unneeded obstacles.

Hallways. Hallways can be a major challenge in a home. Narrow hallways prevent wheelchair access and make it difficult for those using a walker to travel without bumping into walls. Whenever possible, hallways should be eliminated completely, as illustrated in the right drawing below. By using partition walls you can still provide privacy without limiting access. If hallways can't be eliminated, the next best thing is to widen them while also creating a turning radius. For more on a hallway makeover, see pages 68–69 and pages 114–119 on how to widen a hallway.

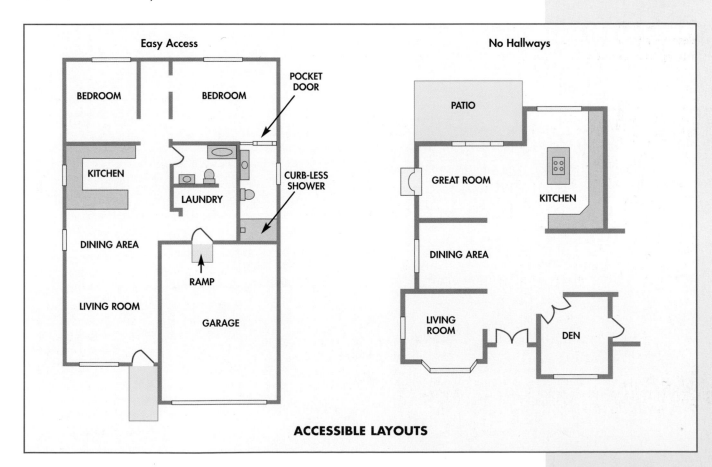

LIVING SPACES GUIDELINES

■ Guidelines for living spaces are much looser than those for the kitchen and bath. The primary area to pay attention to is recommended clearances for halls and doorways. We'll also share some general guidelines for any living space.

Recommended clearances. Housing standards recommend certain clearances throughout a home. The standard width of doorways is 32", with the standard width of all hallways 36"; see the drawing below right. Realize that these are minimums and that many designers try to make doorways and hallways as wide as possible. The proponents of universal design (or barrier-free design)—where spaces are designed to be usable by all people—recommend doorways be a minimum of 36" wide and hallways a minimum of 42" wide. Also, if wheelchair access will be an issue, you'll need to provide at least one 60" turning radius in every hallway.

General guidelines. Any room in the home can be made more accessible by applying these general guidelines.

Flooring: Use non-slip ceramic or vinyl tile, or low-pile, tight-weave carpet. To help define rooms and walkways, consider varying the flooring patterns as shown in the bottom left photo. The high contrast of the carpet "stripe" helps define the dining space and shows a clear path for travel.

Lighting: The best "problem" you can have in a room in terms of lighting is to have too much light. This way you can always draw blinds or drapes or turn off lights. Good lighting helps prevent accidents, and makes a home more comfortable for those with limited eyesight. Remember to replace all wall switches with paddle switches for easier operation.

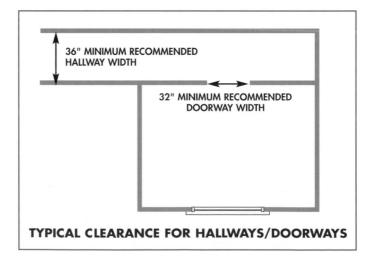

36" MINIMUM RECOMMENDED HALLWAY WIDTH

32" MINIMUM RECOMMENDED DOORWAY WIDTH

TYPICAL CLEARANCE FOR HALLWAYS/DOORWAYS

STORAGE

■ All homes offer some storage space. The question is, how accessible is this space? Many storage units and cabinets don't offer as much access as they could. Some have doors that are hard to open and close, and some are so high you can't reach them. Shown here are solutions to both problems: open shelving and low storage.

Open shelving. One way to make storage space more accessible is to do away with the doors. This way there's no struggling with the door to access the contents of the cabinet. There are three ways to create open shelving: purchase pre-made shelving units, make your own, or simply remove the doors from existing cabinets.

An open shelving unit like the one shown in the kitchen in the top right photo is made by a cabinet manufacturer. These can be ordered individually or in sets from most home centers or can be custom-made by a local cabinetmaker. A less expensive alternative is to make your own open shelving like that shown in the middle photo. This is similar to the open shelving we installed in our master bathroom makeover (see pages 110–111 on how to make your own). Finally, you can simply remove existing doors if they are a barrier. If desired, fill the door hinge mounting holes with putty (just make sure to keep the doors, in case you want to reinstall them at a later date).

Low storage. The handsome window seat shown in the bottom photo invites you to rest, read, and put your feet up. What's really nice is that the built-in storage below is fully accessible. The only thing we'd do to make it more mature-friendly is to replace the small, round knobs with easier-to-use pulls. You don't have to be a woodworker to make a nice-looking storage seat like this. The one here is built from stock cabinets available at most home centers.

Home Plans

You may not plan on building your own accessible home from the ground up, but you definitely can take some tips on modifying your current home from studying specialized home plans. The ones on these pages were originally developed by the North Carolina Cooperative Extension Service, then modified by the Center for Universal Design at North Carolina State University to be fully accessible. (For a complete set of plans, see the order form for the "Accessible Stock House Plans Catalog" at www.design.ncsu.edu/cud/pubs/center/pubslist.htm, or call 919-515-9154.) All of the plans shown here are single-level to provide full access to every room in the home—there are no stairs or steps of any kind.

Plan 1. This modest two-bedroom home offers a large covered porch to provide safe and secure entry at the main door. There are no steps in either the front or rear entry (from the carport to the kitchen). The U-shaped kitchen offers full turning radius for wheelchairs; likewise there's a full turning radius in the master bath, which also has pocket doors for ease of entry from either the bedroom or the short hallway. There is no wall separating the living and dining spaces, so there are no access issues. All in all, a very sweet, simple design.

Plan 2. There's additional space in this three-bedroom, two-bath, ranch-style home. It features an open kitchen/dining/living area that offers a single great room living space. The L-shaped kitchen boasts a full turning radius, as does the adjacent laundry room. The hallway to the bedrooms terminates with an angled door to provide a turning radius here. Both full bathrooms also offer full turning radii as well. (Alternate bathroom designs: a 3' × 3' transfer shower, a roll-in shower in the master bath, or a tub/shower unit with a transfer seat.) Home access is via a separate entry off the carport, and an ample, covered front porch.

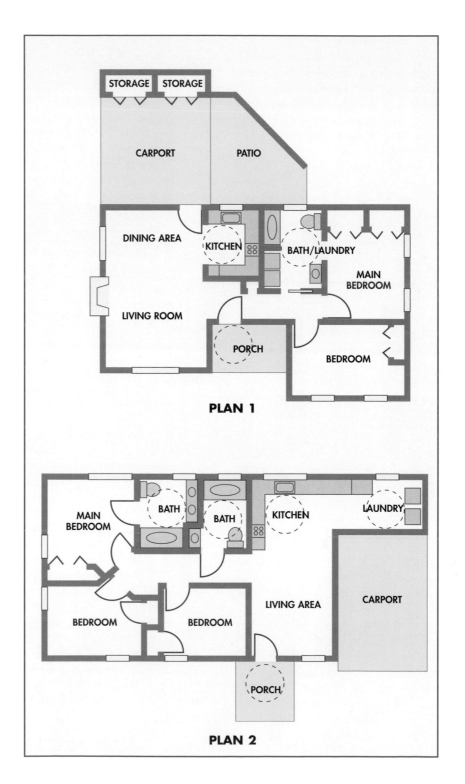

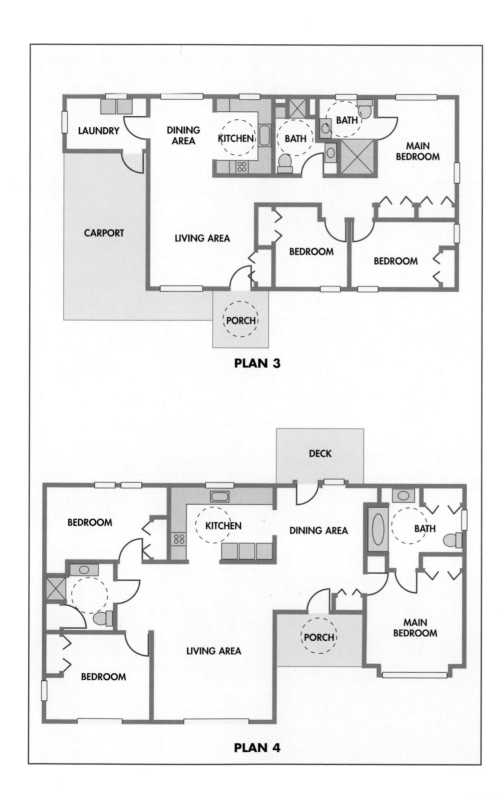

PLAN 3

PLAN 4

Plan 3. Although the dining area flows directly from the living room in the three-bedroom home plan shown here, the kitchen wall helps define space, and creates a sense of separate function between the two rooms. The U-shaped kitchen and each of the two bathrooms offer full turning radii. The master bathroom has a curbless shower for wheel-in access (you could alternatively choose a transfer shower or conventional tub/shower). The wall separating the two smaller bedrooms is shortened to create sufficient turning radius at the end of the hallway. There's a good-sized utility/laundry room off the carport that offers one entry into the home from the rear; the front entry features a covered porch.

Plan 4. The three-bedroom, two-bath plan is an excellent example of a hallway-free home. Access is wide open throughout the entire house. Every room has sufficient turning radius. The L-shaped kitchen also incorporates the laundry room on the opposite wall. For added privacy, a pocket door could be added between the kitchen and the dining room. The baths all have optional layouts (choose 3' × 3' showers, roll-in showers, or conventional tub/shower units). Extra features include built-in desks and storage shelves, to make efficient use of the available space. The front porch is covered and extra-wide; another entry leads from the rear deck into the dining area.

EXTERIOR SPACES

At first glance, it may seem that there's little you can do to the exterior of your home to make it accessible and mature-friendly. Actually, there are a couple of areas that you can change to keep the outside of your aging-in-place home as accommodating as the inside. Two key steps: Eliminate any barriers to access, and replace a hard-to-maintain exterior with a low- or no-maintenance exterior.

Barrier-free access. All three of the homes shown here offer barrier-free access. Although all three houses are multi-level, each has at least one bedroom and a bathroom on the ground floor. Along with the kitchen and living spaces, this creates a single-level living area, a critical aspect of aging in place. Note also that all three homes provide a walkway to the front door that doesn't require stairs. And as shown in the bottom photo, it's obvious that this walkway can be both attractive and functional.

Low- or no-maintenance exterior. Many exteriors are not mature-friendly in that they require constant maintenance, much of which involves climbing ladders and scraping and painting. If your home has a wood exterior, consider moving to aluminum or vinyl siding—both of which are basically maintenance-free. An attractive alternative is to cover all or a portion of the exterior walls in stone. Stone requires little or no maintenance and holds up extremely well over time. The man-made stone veneer shown in the top and bottom photos is from Eldorado Stone (www.eldoradostone.com).

EXTERIOR LAYOUTS

The exterior layout of a home will depend on its original design. There's not a lot you can do to change it that won't require extensive remodeling. The exterior layouts illustrated here, however, show areas that can benefit from accessible and mature-friendly design. The chief target area here is the entryway.

Note that all three of the layouts in the drawing at left offer a covered entryway with ramps in lieu of steps. All three also utilize railings that are decorative and also serve as edge protection. The bottom layout illustrates how you can have both steps and a ramp for access.

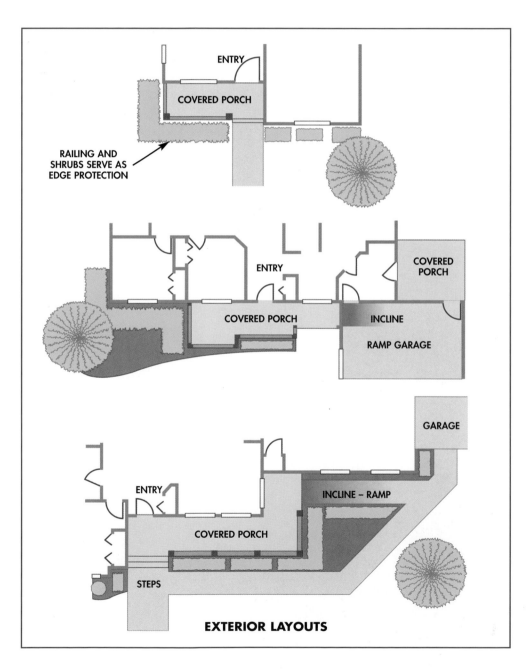

ENTRY

COVERED PORCH

RAILING AND SHRUBS SERVE AS EDGE PROTECTION

ENTRY

COVERED PORCH

COVERED PORCH

INCLINE

RAMP GARAGE

GARAGE

INCLINE – RAMP

ENTRY

COVERED PORCH

STEPS

EXTERIOR LAYOUTS

EXTERIOR GUIDELINES

■ The guidelines for exteriors are few but important. All exterior doors should be a minimum of 36" wide. Porches and walkways should be at least 42" wide; 60" if a turning radius is required. Additionally, the more accessible you can make the entryways, the better. The entryway of a home can create the first barrier. You can eliminate this barrier by creating an entryway with a platform that has no steps and a sufficient turning radius, a railing to serve as edge protection, and a shelf to serve as a landing area for packages, bags, and purses.

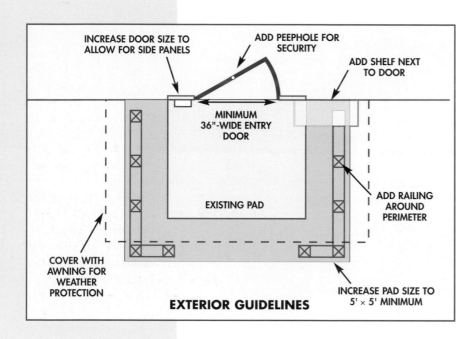

INCREASE DOOR SIZE TO ALLOW FOR SIDE PANELS

ADD PEEPHOLE FOR SECURITY

ADD SHELF NEXT TO DOOR

MINIMUM 36"-WIDE ENTRY DOOR

ADD RAILING AROUND PERIMETER

EXISTING PAD

COVER WITH AWNING FOR WEATHER PROTECTION

INCREASE PAD SIZE TO 5' × 5' MINIMUM

EXTERIOR GUIDELINES

Platform. Many homes have a concrete pad or platform at the base of their entryways. In most cases, these are small and could provide better access if they were enlarged as illustrated in the drawing at left. By increasing the pad to a minimum of 5' × 5', you'll provide sufficient turning radius for a wheelchair.

Railing. A railing constructed partially around the perimeter of the platform or pad can greatly reduce the chances of an accident; see the drawing at left. Alternatively, you can replace the railing with a bench for seating space as well as edge protection. If there's enough room, consider combining a railing with seating. This provides seating, yet offers the higher railing that can also serve as a handrail.

Shelf. At age 22 or 72, when your arms are full of grocery bags, it's tough to open a door. So, a shelf positioned near the entry door will be appreciated by anyone. This handy landing area lets you put down parcels so you can unlock and/or operate the door handset without worrying about dropping what you're carrying as you fumble for keys. There are a number of simple shelves you can build, as illustrated in the bottom drawing.

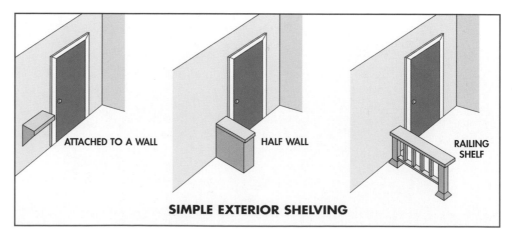

ATTACHED TO A WALL

HALF WALL

RAILING SHELF

SIMPLE EXTERIOR SHELVING

WORKING WITH PROS

■ Although many homeowners hesitate to call in a design pro to help with a project because of the cost, they're usually surprised to find out that they end up saving money. That's because a knowledgeable pro often makes suggestions that will save money in the short run and prevent headaches in the long run.

Professional designers and decorators have access to materials and products that are available "to the trade only"—not to the public. So, they can obtain goods that you're not likely to see in your neighbor's house. And in working with these goods, professionals gain experience with style, color, and pattern that can help you avoid an unfortunate selection.

Here's where professionals really shine: They're better than most of us at seeing the big picture. For instance, a designer might find an elegant solution to traffic-flow jams or cramped spaces by recommending that you move a wall—something the average home-owner may not consider.

Working with a design professional doesn't have to mean hiring her or him to do your entire makeover—you might engage someone on an à la carte basis to help select a theme or color scheme. You could, for example, hire a pro to create a color board like the one shown in the bottom photo. A color board brings the major elements of a design together in one place so you can see how the elements do or don't work together. The color board shown below was created by the design pros at Timberlake Cabinet Company for the kitchen makeover shown on pages 71–72. On the nuts-and-bolts side, a decorator or designer can help you source contractors if you need them. If you do work with a professional, be sure to check their references, and get a written quote for their work. Make sure both of you under-stand exactly what services will be provided, and put the agreement in writing.

Kitchen makeovers. If you're planning on new cabinets as part of your kitchen makeover, consider getting professional help with the design—even if you plan on installing the cabinets yourself. There are several good reasons to do this. First, a kitchen designer has access to all the major cabinet manufacturers and will know which is best for you. Second, they'll ask you a lot of questions about how you cook, how many cooks there are, size of family, type of cooking, etc. Then, given your budget and space limitations and any physical concerns, they'll design your kitchen. Most designers use high-tech CAD (computer-aided drafting) programs for this, so they can show you exactly what your kitchen will look like. What's really nice about this is they can change details (such as cabinet style) with a single mouse-click—even adding or subtracting a cabinet is no big deal. Third, they'll be able to generate an order list that will specify everything you need, from crown molding to filler strips.

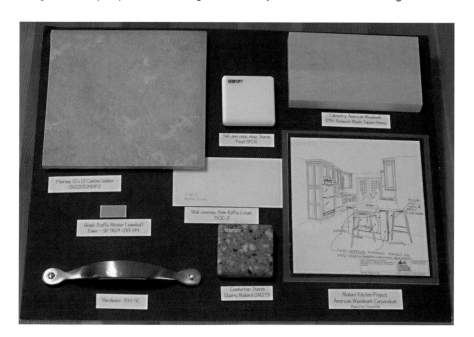

WINDOWS AND DOORS

■ The windows and doors of an accessible or aging-in-place home should have a few major attributes: They should be functional, easy to operate, and attractive.

Function. The function of a door or window will depend on the room it's in and what you want it to do. Not all windows open; the acrylic-block windows shown in the middle photo let in light while still affording privacy. The large picture-style windows shown in the top photo also do not open, but provide a panoramic view. If you're planning on replacing windows as part of a makeover, read the section below before making a purchase.

Ease of operation. Depending on the size of the window, opening or closing a window can require considerable strength. The classic double-hung window requires you to lift the bottom sash to open the window. Even windows equipped with sash weights or springs can be hard to operate. Sliding windows have similar problems. If you do need to replace windows, we recommend you go with casement windows. These windows open and close via a hand crank—no lifting or sliding required. And what's best is that you can operate them from a wheelchair. For more on casement windows and how to install them, see pages 48 and 144–145, respectively.

Appearance. Appearance is a matter of personal taste. A window or door that's attractive to one homeowner may be hideous to another. The good news is that there are almost as many styles and choices in windows and doors as there are homeowners. Instead of clear glass, consider going with frosted or art glass like that installed in the door in the bottom photo. Frosted and art glass offer additional privacy while still allowing in light. Specialty glass can be used in both windows and doors; we added art glass inserts in the pocket doors installed in our kitchen makeover as shown on pages 71–72. Inserts like the one shown on page 71 are available from ODL (www.odl.com).

LIGHTING

For most folks, the more light a home has, the better. This is especially true for people with aging eyes or vision loss: Whether natural or artificial, good lighting will help us see better. This not only makes day-to-day living easier, but it also enhances safety: When objects in a room can be seen clearly, accidents are less likely.

Natural light. Natural light, of course, is what nature brings us via the sun. It makes plants grow, chases away seasonal depression, and fills our living spaces with a bright, well…light feeling. Natural light helps our homes feel open and spacious, and helps illuminate our whole lives. If you need more windows or larger windows to feel comfortable in your home, consider giving up a little wall space for the added light. Alternatively, consider skylights, as they can bring in a lot more light without touching an inch of living space.

Artificial light began with the first fire lit in a cave, but it's still a relative new-comer. Today, we group artificial light into three categories: general, like a ceiling fixture in a dining room; task, such as a reading light on an end table; or accent, as when a recessed light showcases a shelf of collectibles.

General lighting. General lighting is what lets us use and move around a room safely. In the past, general lighting was an incandescent or fluorescent overhead. Now, design trends lean toward recessed lighting (top right photo).

Task lighting. Task lighting is self-explanatory: It puts light where you need it to perform tasks, like the work areas and countertops shown in the middle photo. While recessed lights positioned over a countertop do provide some light, under-cabinet lights do the job better. These are usually either strip or single "puck" halogen lights. They're often low-voltage and can be installed with ease (see page 177).

Accent lighting. When you want to showcase a feature in a room, turn on decorative or accent lighting. It doesn't matter whether you're displaying the grandkids' ventures in ceramics or a favorite artist's creation with a wall sconce, as in the bottom photo. Whatever the object to be accented, just pressing a switch can create a completely different look or mood.

COLOR

As you probably know, color affects many aspects of our lives. It can influence mood (bright yellow is cheery), shape perception (doesn't the room look bigger in pale green!), and stimulate appetites (this red wallpaper is making me hungry). With all that power, color has yet another role to play for an older population: safety. Yes, safety. When eyes need help in picking out room details, color can answer the call.

Not exactly sure where the chair edge is, or where the countertop ends and the cooktop begins? Color can be the cue here and in so many places, helping define features and areas...and helping avoid accidents. "High contrast" among the colors of home materials is a prime objective. So, for a mature-friendly makeover, this can be the perfect time to go wild (or a bit wilder) with color choices.

On these pages, you'll find examples of how color can enhance aging in place, in everything from countertops to commodes.

Countertops. Gorgeous blue countertop? Sure. But this solid-surface choice also offers an easy-to-see, high visual contrast with the wood cabinets and gas cooktop.

Furniture and accents. You've always loved apricot and blue? Now's the time to pair them with textiles, upholstery, and carpet that make a vivid, high-contrast, eye-catching setting.

Wall treatments. We've all walked into walls. But when the walls are apple green against a dark floor, older eyes are more apt to detect them sooner, and avoid a nasty bump.

Flooring. You can't overlook this knockout red carpet, or the way the cream-colored furnishings stand out on it. So, there's no doubt where to sit and walk safely.

Color is a personal choice. Still, there are some color basics to keep in mind that will keep that screaming red from sending you from the room screaming.

The three primary colors are red, yellow, and blue: These are used to mix all of the other colors. The secondary colors are orange, green, and violet: They are mixed from equal parts of two primaries. In between there are intermediate colors; see the color wheel at right. If you want to select a contrast color (as a trim accent, let's say), choose a color that's opposite it on the color wheel. For example, a contrast to blue is orange. On the other hand, to find colors that will blend well, choose adjacent colors (such as yellow-green and green). Soft pastels are the result of mixing white with one of these pure colors.

Know, too, that colors look different in different types of light. Incandescents (common lightbulbs) emphasize reds and yellows. Fluorescents highlight blues. That's why it's so important to examine paint chips and wallpaper samples in your home to see how they look in a target room before deciding on a color; never choose these at the home center. Consider, too, how much of a color you'll be using. Deep purple may look great as a trim paint accent, but overpowering on a whole wall. Finally, remember that color is affected by colors around it. So, hold chips next to each other before making selections.

Fixtures. Even if black isn't your vision for a bathroom makeover, it's easy to see how fixture colors can make a really strong visual difference. (A nice blue would work, too.)

To really make your best color choices, be familiar with the three kinds of color schemes: monochromatic, analogous, and complementary. A monochromatic scheme uses shades and intensities of a single color—say, blue. An analogous theme combines variations of colors that are close to each other on the color wheel, such as yellow, yellow-orange, and orange. A complementary theme uses combinations of complementary colors like red and green.

Since colors create moods, it's often best to begin by picking the primary "mood" you're after, and its corresponding color. For a warm "feel," go with reds, oranges, and yellows. For a cool, peaceful effect, choose soft greens and blues. To go bold and flashy, choose contrasting colors. If it all seems overwhelming, go to the paint aisle and say "Help!" There are hundreds of professionally selected color palettes to guide your choices. They'll get you off to an excellent start.

Cabinets. Nothing bland here—just an ocean of marine blue. The reflective stainless steel counters and fixtures offer enough visual contrast to be clearly seen.

Appliances. The heck with resale neutrals: If you want a red refrigerator, go for it—especially with a bottom-freezer model that eliminates tiptoe reaching.

2

CHOOSING MATERIALS

When your home needs updating to keep up with your life stage, the materials you choose can be more important than for any other type of makeover. This is because the choices you make can mean the difference between being able to use the materials and not. For example: You buy an elongated, raised-height toilet for a bathroom, and have the old toilet removed. There you are (maybe with a plumber or helper), ready for the installation, but there's a problem: The new toilet won't fit into the existing plumbing. There goes your makeover budget.

That's why it's so important to learn about materials and products on the market—and more importantly, what's accessible and mature-friendly that will work for you. And don't think that you have to sacrifice looks for function: The wall-mounted sink on the opposite page is proof. This glass beauty provides wheelchair access.

FLOORING

To choose flooring wisely for the various rooms in your accessible home, you'll need to know which flooring works best in each type of room and what types of flooring to avoid entirely. Here are the facts you need to choose what will work best for you.

Kitchens, bathrooms, and entryways. Some of the hardest-working floors in your home are in the kitchen, bathrooms, and entryways. That's because each of these can and often does come in contact with water. Flooring that holds up well to water includes ceramic and vinyl tile, as shown in the top and middle photos.

Ceramic tile is easy for do-it-yourselfers because it's easy to recut a tile if you make a mistake. Choose a floor tile that has a matte or textured finish, and avoid glossy tiles; they're slippery underfoot. There are a few disadvantages to ceramic tile floors. First, they don't offer any "give" and so can be hard on the feet. Second, the hard tile is cold, "noisy," and unforgiving if you drop a dish or glass. An attractive version of ceramic tile is mosaic tile. These small ceramic tiles (1" × 1" or larger) are bonded to a backing to make 12" sheets that are easy to install. Because of the flexible backing, mosaics are more forgiving of uneven floors.

Regardless of the color, pattern, or texture, all sheet vinyl is one of two types: full-spread or perimeter-bond. Full-spread flooring has a felt-paper backing and is designed for the entire surface to be glued to the subfloor or underlayment with flooring adhesive, as described on pages 80–81. Perimeter-bond flooring has a smooth, white PVC backing that is secured to the floor only at the perimeter with staples. Because it has no backing, perimeter-bond flooring has some give-and-take, so it can be stretched slightly during installation.

Living spaces. Although you can install ceramic or vinyl tile in living spaces, most people prefer the warmth and softness that carpet offers. Carpet is offered in a dizzying variety of colors and patterns (bottom photo). But do you know about the different types of carpeting available? The four most common are: cushion-backed carpet, where the carpet has a foam backing bonded to it; loop-pile carpet that provides a textured look, resulting from the uncut loops of yarn; plush carpet, with the pile trimmed at a bevel; and velvet-cut pile carpet, which offers the densest pile of all.

For an accessible and mature-friendly home, you want a low-nap or low-pile carpet that's fairly dense. The lower, dense nap helps prevent tripping and is easier to move across with a walker or wheelchair. One excellent choice is carpet made with Honeywell Anso nylon: It's soft and durable, is easy to maintain, and resists stains and soiling (www.ansonylon.com).

Flooring to avoid. Because of its slick surface, steer clear of wood flooring and any laminate flooring that comes in a glossy finish. If you do decide to use laminate flooring, avoid using it in rooms where water can damage it, such as a kitchen or bathroom. Even if you seal the joints with glue, water can still seep in and damage the flooring. Finally, do not use throw rugs of any kind in any room. These are one of the major causes of falls and injuries.

CABINET HARDWARE AND ACCESSORIES

■ Choosing the correct cabinet hardware and accessories can make the difference between easily accessing the contents of the cabinet and struggling to do so.

Cabinet hardware. When it comes to choosing cabinet hardware, think pulls, not knobs. Knobs of any size require you to wrap your fingers around the knob to pull it. As we age, not only does it become difficult to grip round objects, but also we often lack the strength needed to pull the knob. Here's where pulls come in (like those shown in the top photo). What you're looking for is a pull that's large enough to let you slip your fingers behind the pull. This way you can open a door without having to grip anything. For step-by-step directions on how to replace existing cabinet hardware or install new hardware, see page 105.

ACCESSIBLE ACCESSORIES

■ There are numerous cabinet accessories available from both cabinet manufacturers and accessory manufacturers (like Rev-A-Shelf, www.rev-a-shelf.com) that bring cabinet contents conveniently out to you.

Pivot-out bins. These two-part pivoting bins attach to the door and cabinet interior so that as the door is opened, the lid rises and the bin conveniently pivots out.

Pull-out bins. Similar to a full-extension slide for a drawer, a large slide attaches inside the cabinet base. The cabinet door mounts directly to the slide and the bin is accessed by pulling the door.

Pull-down shelving. A relative newcomer, this ingenious shelving rack mounts to the inside bottom of the cabinet and pivots down to put the contents within easy reach.

Pull-out shelving. If you've ever been on hands and knees to rummage in a cabinet, you'll appreciate these pull-out shelves; one half of the shelf slide screws to the cabinet, the other to the shelf or tray.

CABINETS

If you're planning to replace some or all of the cabinets in your kitchen or other room in your home, you'll need to know a bit about how cabinets are made and what they're made of to make your wisest buying decision.

Cabinet types. There are two basic types of cabinets available, face frame and frameless, as illustrated in the bottom drawing. On a face frame cabinet, the sides, back, top, and bottom are made of thin material joined together with glue and staples. The cabinet strength comes from a solid-wood frame that's attached to the front of the cabinet, as shown in the top photo. Doors and drawers are then cut to fit the openings. Because the face frame reduces the size of the openings, there is less interior storage space—especially for drawers. On the plus side, face frame cabinets are the easiest to install because any gaps can be filled with filler strips (see page 95 for more on these). The frame parts on quality cabinets are joined with mortises and tenons, or at the very least, dowels.

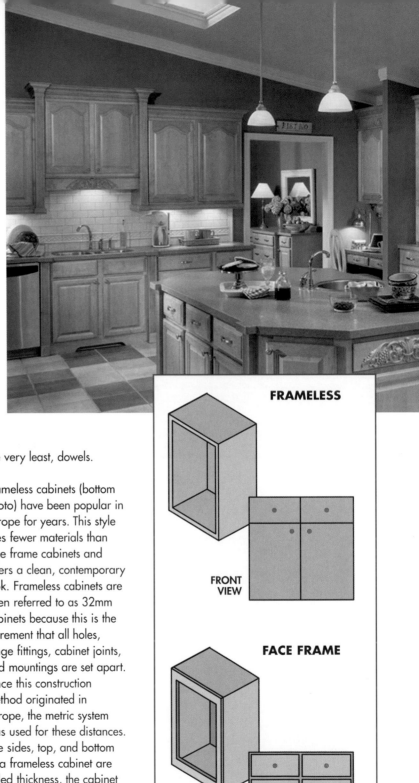

Frameless cabinets (bottom photo) have been popular in Europe for years. This style uses fewer materials than face frame cabinets and offers a clean, contemporary look. Frameless cabinets are often referred to as 32mm cabinets because this is the increment that all holes, hinge fittings, cabinet joints, and mountings are set apart. Since this construction method originated in Europe, the metric system was used for these distances. The sides, top, and bottom of a frameless cabinet are typically made of ¾"-thick particleboard. Because of this added thickness, the cabinet parts when assembled are sufficiently strong and do not need a face frame to provide support. This opens up the full interior space for storage. Doors are mounted via fully adjustable hinges that attach to the inside of the cabinet.

Ordering options. When it's time to order your new cabinets, you'll find there are three basic types to choose from: stock, semi-custom, and custom. Stock cabinets are constructed either in advance or on an on-demand basis. Most stock cabinet manufacturers offer a wide array of sizes and styles. These are the least expensive of the cabinets, and delivery is usually quick. The disadvantage to these is that you're limited to the sizes they offer. Semi-custom manufacturers do make some stock cabinets, but most are made on an on-demand basis. You'll find a wider choice of cabinet sizes and styles. Custom cabinets are all made to order and there is no warehouse full of cabinets. This means a significant wait between the order and delivery. But custom cabinetmakers offer superior materials and construction methods.

ACCESSIBLE CABINETS

■ Many of the leading cabinet manufacturers are starting to offer cabinets that are accessible and mature-friendly. Most common features are pull-out work surfaces, tambour-style fronts, and recessed base cabinets.

Pull-out work surfaces. For those seated in a wheelchair, food prep can often be a challenge. Now, though, the process can be easier with a convenient, pull-out work surface. On some models, the top tray can be removed to access the contents below.

Tambour-style fronts. Opening and closing doors to access cabinet contents is no longer an issue when the cabinet front sports a tambour roll-up like the one shown here.

Recessed base cabinets. Washing dishes or cooking on a cooktop can be a hassle for the cook in a wheelchair. By simply having the sink base or cooktop base recessed, the cook can roll up closer.

COUNTERTOPS

■ If part of your makeover includes replacing kitchen or bathroom countertops, you'll need to know the pros and cons of the various choices available. Although plastic laminate has been the prevailing countertop for many years (and it's still a good choice), it's steadily being replaced by solid-surface countertops such as Samsung Staron, Corian, and Silestone.

Plastic laminate. This super-tough material is made of several layers of resin-impregnated paper bonded to a colorful top layer of paper and then covered with clear melamine plastic. This is then bonded to a particleboard core that may or may not have a backsplash. Plastic laminate's well-deserved reputation for durability combined with low cost and easy cleanup make this an excellent choice for makeovers on a tight budget.

Solid-surface materials. Solid-surface material (such as Staron: www.getstaron.com) is made from acrylic resins and mineral fillers that are formed into ½"-thick sheets for countertops (top photo). You can even get sinks made out of this stuff: When bonded to the countertop, no seams will show (middle photo). Solid-surface countertops are easy to clean and water-resistant, and unlike thin laminate, you can sand out blemishes in this thicker top. On the downside, this material does stain more readily than plastic laminate, costs more, and usually requires professional installation. Because these countertops are solid all the way through, the edges can be milled to any profile, the top can be routed for drainage, and recesses can be made to accept decorative inlays for a truly unique look. This is particularly useful for creating softened edges that are safer to bump into, like the sink edges shown in the bottom photo.

Ceramic tile. Ceramic tile is one of the most do-it-yourself-friendly materials for countertops. Individual tiles are more forgiving than a large sheet of plastic laminate or solid-surface material. If you mess up a tile, just cut another. Ceramic tiles are inexpensive and are available in a huge assortment of colors, shapes, sizes, and textures. When installed correctly, they're heat-proof, scratch- and water-resistant, and long-lasting. The disadvantage to a ceramic tile countertop is the grout—it stains easily and is difficult to keep clean.

TRUE SELF-RIMMING

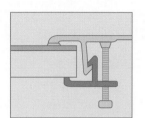

SELF-RIMMING WITH CLIPS

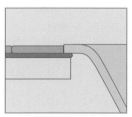

FLUSH WITH TILE

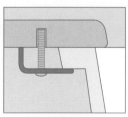

UNDER-COUNTER

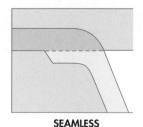

SEAMLESS

KITCHEN SINKS AND FAUCETS

■ The kitchen sink is the most-used plumbing fixture in your home. So, choosing one that will serve you well and provide the look and feel you're after takes some thought. In order of importance, you'll need to choose how the sink is mounted, what it's made of, the number and size of bowls—and of course, the color and style. Kitchen sinks are typically classified by how they are mounted: true self-rimming, self-rimming with clips, flush with tile, under-counter, and seamless, as illustrated in the drawing at left.

Sink materials. Once you've decided on the mounting style, it's time to select the material. The most common choices are stainless steel, porcelain over cast iron, and composite or solid surface. Stainless steel sinks (top photo) are virtually free from staining and can be buffed out when scratched. Stainless steel sinks are relatively inexpensive and are easy to find and install. Cast iron sinks are quiet and massive, with a tough porcelain coating. But cast iron sinks are not flexible; if you drop a dish in one, the dish will likely break. And the porcelain surface, although hard, can be chipped easily if a metal knife or pot is dropped in the sink. Composite sinks (middle photo) can be glued to the underside of the countertop with special adhesives that will create a virtually seamless seam. Not only does this eliminate the possibility of leaks, but it also creates smooth-flowing lines and a rimless sink: There's no edge to capture food particles, no edge to interfere with wiping off the countertop.

Number of and size of bowls. Bowls vary from one to three, and they can be identical in size and depth, or vary. Deeper-bowl sinks are popular, as well as sinks with a smaller bowl inset between two larger bowls. The smaller middle bowl frequently has a garbage disposal attached to it. Bowl number and size is really a matter of personal preference—if you pick a larger sink, just make sure that it fits in your countertop.

Faucets. A sink faucet in an accessible kitchen should have the following features: It should have an easy-to-maintain and -clean surface, it should have a pull-out sprayer, and most important, the control should be a single handle, as shown in the bottom photo. Alternatively, if you prefer separate handles, make sure to choose lever-style handles like those shown on pages 154–155.

APPLIANCES

If new appliances are part of your makeover, take the time up front to select them—especially if new cabinets are being installed. There's not a cabinet designer out there who will start a job until you've first selected the appliances. That's because the cabinets are designed to fit around them. If you did it the other way 'round, you'd be faced with selecting appliances by size, and odds are you wouldn't end up with the features you want. Unfortunately, this is often what happens with a makeover where the cabinets are unchanged, except maybe for appearance (painting, refacing, etc.). If this is the case for you, carefully measure the existing appliance opening and use these measurements to narrow down your choices.

Dishwashers. The dishwasher is one of the few appliances that's fairly standard in dimensions: Most fit in a 24"-wide space under a countertop. Dishwashers come in two types: front-loading and pull-out drawers. You can make a front-loading dishwasher mature-friendly by raising it up from the floor, as shown in the photo at right. This reduces the amount of bending for anyone, whether seated in a wheelchair or standing. Drawer-style dishwashers like the one shown in the top right photo are relatively new and offer the convenience of slide-out drawers that can be used independently. These, too, can be raised up off the floor.

Refrigerators. Years ago, most refrigerators were a standard size. But homeowners have asked for increasingly larger food-storage space. Manufacturers have responded by making larger and larger units. Regardless of the door configuration (side by side or top and bottom), note that in addition to being wider and taller, many larger units are deeper, too. Unless the refrigerator is installed into a built-in alcove, the extra depth will make the refrigerator stick out considerably past any adjacent countertops. In response to this, some makers are building counter-depth units. Another way to mask this extra depth is to install a built-in refrigerator, where the cabinetry is brought out flush with the doors of the unit (top left photo on the opposite page). Side-by-side refrigerators are considered mature-friendly since you can access both the refrigerator and freezer while either seated in a wheelchair or standing. Some appliance manufacturers now offer top and bottom

units with the freezer on the bottom, as shown in the bottom left photo on the opposite page. Because the freezer is accessed by pulling out a drawer at the bottom, both the refrigerator and freezer are also accessible to those standing or seated.

Cooktops and wall ovens. When it comes time to choose appliances for cooking, steer away from ranges if possible. Although ranges combine a cooktop and oven in a single unit, they're not mature-friendly. This is obvious if you've ever had to lift a heavy roasting pan from the bottom of the oven. And, cooks in wheelchairs have to place their chair parallel to the cooktop and reach over the side of the chair—a very awkward and potentially dangerous situation. The optimum cooking appliances in a mature-friendly kitchen are a separate cooktop and wall oven.

As soon as you separate the oven from the cooktop, it opens up several installation possibilities that didn't exist before. That's because a cooktop by itself is only a few inches deep. This means you can install one almost anywhere—in islands, peninsulas, etc. (bottom left photo). And more importantly, you can recess the cabinet below the cooktop for wheelchair access, as described on page 97. This means a cook in a wheelchair can pull up directly in front of the cooktop and enjoy full access. Look for cooktops with up-front controls with large, easy-to-operate knobs. Separating the cooktop and oven also means that wall ovens can be installed higher, at a comfortable working height (top right photo). Not only does this make it much easier to use, but it also lets you keep an eye on the food without bending over. Wall ovens are available in single or double units; some are available with microwave ovens as well.

Laundry. Washers and dryers have changed dramatically over the years, and now most appliance manufacturers offer units that can be loaded from the front (bottom right photo) instead of from the top. This makes them much more mature-friendly, as there's no reaching up and over to get at clothes. Look for front-loading units with simple and easy-to-use controls that are also up front. You can make these machines even easier to use by placing them on pedestals or a homemade platform.

If you do make a platform, use stout lumber and rigid construction.

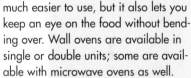

BATHROOM SINKS AND FAUCETS

As the bathroom fixture that gets the most use, a sink may deserve the most care and planning. It must serve your needs, fit in with the design style of the room, and have a color that will please the eye for years. To select a new sink, consider how it's mounted and what it's made of. After that come the choices in color and style. Bathroom sinks are defined by how they're mounted: drop-in, under-counter, above-counter, integral, wall-mount, and pedestal.

Sink mounting options. To create the best access, a mature-friendly sink should be wall-mounted or semi-mounted. Both of these mounting options allow for wheelchair access. Any sink that is solely supported by a wall is considered a wall-mount sink. These sinks attach directly to the wall or hang on a bracket attached to the wall (top photo). Although wall-mount sinks offer plenty of leg space, the plumbing lines can be visible. Some manufacturers (like American Standard: www.americanstandard.com) offer wall-mount sinks with integral covers to hide exposed plumbing—we used one of these for the guest bathroom makeover shown on page 63. Another way to hide plumbing lines is with a semi-mount sink. These are a hybrid of a drop-in sink and a wall-mount sink; we used a semi-mount sink in the master bathroom makeover shown on page 65.

Sink materials. Most bathroom sinks are porcelain or vitreous china or made from a composite. A vitreous china sink is made of ceramic/porcelain that has been "vitrified" to create a glasslike surface that absorbs less water than most other ceramics. These are inexpensive and easy to maintain and come in the widest variety of shapes, sizes, and colors. Composite sinks (bottom photo) are fairly new and, like composite kitchen sinks, they can be glued to the underside of the countertop with special adhesives that create a virtually undetectable seam.

Bathroom faucets. Bathroom faucets come in an enormous array of styles, handle options, and finishes. Handle options include single and separate handles. Which configuration you choose is really a matter of personal preference. What's important is to make sure the faucet has easy-to-operate lever-style handles, like those shown in the middle photo. For more on lever-style faucets, see pages 154–155.

BATHTUBS AND SHOWERS

■ There aren't many things more personal than bathing. As we age, maintaining personal hygiene can become difficult—and that can lead to very real emotional distress, on top of health issues. If you have only a traditional bathtub/shower in the home, getting in and out safely can take great care; slips can be disastrous. Fortunately, a growing number of bathing fixture manufacturers acknowledge this, and have started making showers and bathtubs that are easy and safe to use. Showers can be either curb-less or have low thresholds; bathtubs can have doors—yes, doors—so you can walk right in. Regardless of what type of tub or shower you have or choose to install, make sure to add grab bars; see pages 46 and 165.

Showers. Standard shower units have relatively high thresholds that can be difficult to safely step over. Smart fixture manufacturers like Lasco Bathware (www.lascobathware.com) make shower units with lower thresholds, as shown in the middle photo. These units can be recessed into the floor to create a barrier-free or curb-less shower. Another form of curb-less shower is the built-in variety, like the one shown in the top photo. Built-in tiled showers like these are best installed by a tile pro.

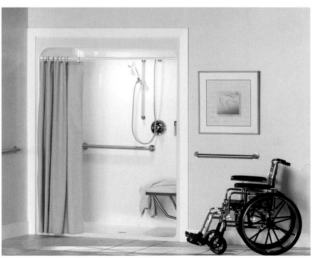

Shower units come in single or multiple pieces. Multi-piece units are easy to transport and install, as the pieces basically bolt together. A note of caution about one-piece molded shower or tub/shower surrounds: Measure your space—and your doorway—carefully. These units are big, and designed mostly for use in new construction. You don't want to bring home the shower of your dreams, only to find it won't fit through the bathroom door. For more on installing a one-piece shower unit, see pages 169–171.

Bathtubs. A walk-in bathtub has the power to change lives. This may sound overstated, but it's true. The ability to keep yourself clean has a huge impact on attitude, outlook, and personal well-being. When folks with limited physical abilities who've had to curtail routine hygiene can safely bathe again, they universally report that they feel like new people, happier people. BathEase (www.bathease.com), the manufacturer of the walk-in tub shown in the bottom photo and featured in our guest bathroom makeover (page 63), offers many product options. You can choose from a number of styles and sizes, including units with built-in seats and jetted sprays, available with or without shower walls.

GRAB BARS

When most people think about grab bars, they envision those heavy-duty, metal units found in most hospitals and elder-care facilities. That view is outdated: Grab bars don't have to be unattractive. (There's also research indicating that metal bars promote the spread of bacteria.) The grab bars shown in the side-bar below are made of an anti-bacterial, thick nylon bonded to aluminum, manufactured and marketed by Safe-Access Systems, Inc. (www.pba-na.com), under exclusive license from PBA.

When shopping for grab bars and rails, look for units that have secure mounting hardware. They should also be durable, strong, non-slip, and fire- and electricity-safe. The bath safety products and accessories available from Safe-Access Systems are offered in several different colors, so you can match them to your existing fixtures. One good example: the grab bar we installed that blends right in with the walk-in bathtub shown on page 166.

TYPES OF GRAB BARS

Stationary. Grab bars that are mounted permanently to the wall are termed stationary. This is a very secure mounting method, but the bar (left of the sink) is fixed and cannot be moved out of the way if needed.

Fold-up. Grab bars that fold up or down or rotate to pivot out of the way offer support only when you need it. The unit shown here folds up and then rotates to store flat against the wall.

Grab bar accessories. For maximum choice, some grab bar manufacturers also offer matching accessories, like the handheld showerhead and suspended shower seat shown here.

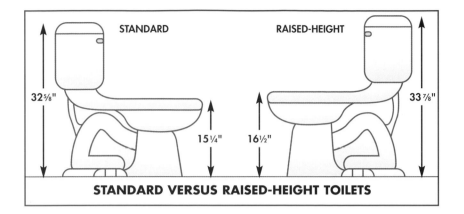

STANDARD **RAISED-HEIGHT**

32⅝"   33⅞"

15¼" 16½"

STANDARD VERSUS RAISED-HEIGHT TOILETS

TOILETS

■ Choosing a toilet for a mature-friendly bathroom is fairly simple. You're looking for one of three toilet types: a raised-height toilet, a wall-hung toilet, or an in-wall tank toilet. You'll also need to choose from the flushing actions available, as well as fixture color.

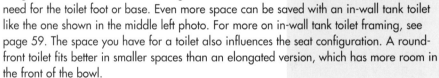

Raised-height toilets. It's surprising how much difference a couple of inches can make. That's all the difference in height there is between a standard and a raised-height toilet, as illustrated in the drawing above and the photo at right. But just these few inches have a big impact on the ease of sitting down on or getting up from a toilet. Raised-height toilets have become so popular that many fixture manufacturers offer most of their styles at this height.

Space-saving toilets. Especially in small bathrooms, a couple of inches here or there can mean the difference between being able to use the facilities and not. A wall-hung toilet mounts to the wall framing and removes the need for the toilet foot or base. Even more space can be saved with an in-wall tank toilet like the one shown in the middle left photo. For more on in-wall tank toilet framing, see page 59. The space you have for a toilet also influences the seat configuration. A round-front toilet fits better in smaller spaces than an elongated version, which has more room in the front of the bowl.

Flushing action. In this era of choice, you can even select the flushing action of your new toilet: wash-down, reverse-trap, siphon-jet, ultra-low flush, and pressure-assist, as illustrated in the drawing below. Wash-down traps are inexpensive and simple, but noisy. The trap is at the front of the bowl and is flushed by streams of water draining from the rim. A reverse-trap toilet is similar to a wash-down toilet but the trap is at the rear of the bowl. This makes the bowl longer but provides for a quieter flush. On a siphon-jet toilet, the trap is at the rear and a small hole in the bottom sends a jet of water into the trap to create a siphoning action when flushed. In addition to being quiet, siphon-jet toilets also provide a large water-surface area. Similar to a reverse-trap toilet, an ultra-low flush has a lower water table and correspondingly small surface area. This allows for a smaller tank and less water per flush. In a pressure-assisted toilet, the water supply is used to compress air, which creates a "push-through" flush. These are very efficient, but are more expensive and can be noisy.

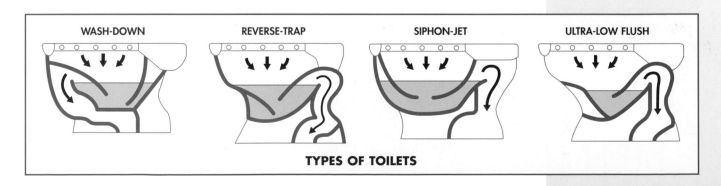

WASH-DOWN   **REVERSE-TRAP**   **SIPHON-JET**   **ULTRA-LOW FLUSH**

TYPES OF TOILETS

WINDOWS AND DOORS

■ When it comes to buying new or replacement windows for a mature-friendly home, there are really only a couple of features necessary. With windows, make sure they are crank-operated casement windows. For exterior doors, if space is available, select a door that has side view panels (to see who's at your door), and make sure the handsets are lever-operated for ease of use.

Casement windows. A casement window is any window where the sash is hinged on the side to allow it to pivot in and out like a door. Most casement windows project outward and therefore provide significantly better ventilation than sliding windows of equal size. Extra ventilation is nice, but the big deal about casement windows is that they open and close via a hand crank (middle photo). Unlike single- and double-hung or sliding windows, which can require significant physical strength and dexterity to operate, a single crank lets you open or close a window with little effort—whether seated or standing. Look for energy-efficient windows with double panes and preferably a low-E coating. The coating filters out UV rays to protect furnishings, while also helping to insulate the home against cold and heat.

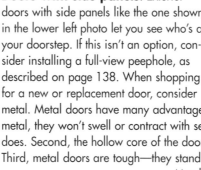

Doors with side panels. Exterior doors with side panels like the one shown in the lower left photo let you see who's at your doorstep. If this isn't an option, consider installing a full-view peephole, as described on page 138. When shopping for a new or replacement door, consider metal. Metal doors have many advantages over solid-wood doors. First, since they're metal, they won't swell or contract with seasonal changes in humidity as a wood door does. Second, the hollow core of the door can be filled with foam to provide insulation. Third, metal doors are tough—they stand up extremely well to regular use (and abuse). Metal doors are available in a multitude of shapes and sizes and can even be found covered with a wood veneer to give the appearance of solid wood.

Lever-style handsets. All of the doors in a mature-friendly home should have lever-style handsets, like the one shown in the bottom photo. Unlike a knob, the handsets can be operated without having to grasp the lever. You can open a door with a closed fist if necessary.

WALL COVERINGS

To update your wall coverings, the smart choices are much the same as for most makeovers: They include paint, wallpaper, ceramic tile, and tileboard. What makes each of these mature-friendly is that they're easy to apply, and they hold up well over time.

Wallpaper. Wallpaper is an excellent choice for many rooms of the home (top right photo). Vinyl wallpaper is great for kitchens as it's fairly impervious to stains. Wallpaper comes in many patterns and colors, but takes more time to apply than paint. Some wallpapers also offer textures that simulate surfaces such as bamboo or woven cloth. When shopping for wallpaper, choose the strippable variety: You'll appreciate it when it comes time to remove it for a new look.

Paint. Paint is by far the simplest wall covering in the home (middle photo). Its biggest advantage is that it's so easy to change if you want a new look—just brush on a new coat. To make cleanup easier, choose a satin- or eggshell-finish latex paint. Avoid flat paints as they are tougher to keep clean. Some specialty paints provide texture, such as suede, and faux finishes like ragging can create the look of texture.

Ceramic tile. Ceramic tile is one of the hardiest coverings for kitchens and baths (lower right photo). It's stain-resistant, easy to clean, and easy to install. Four-inch tiles and smaller mosaic tiles work best for this, and they also come in many colors, patterns, and textures. An inexpensive way to add a nice accent is to install a hand-made or sculpted tile at regular intervals. These specialty tiles can be quite expensive but are affordable in small quantities.

Tileboard. Tileboard is a beautiful, durable, and cost-effective option for wall coverings. Tileboard is often referred to as wallboard, wall paneling, or a decorative wall covering. It's easy to install (see pages 124–125), and some types are moisture-resistant. What's best is that once installed, it's virtually maintenance-free. The handsome tileboard shown in the bottom photo and used in our guest bathroom makeover (page 63) is manufactured by DPI (www.decpanels.com).

LIGHTING

■ The ability to see clearly is a major aspect of maintaining independence and quality of life. For mature people, though, simply adding light may not be the answer. When too much of the wrong type of light is used to combat vision loss, the resulting glare can create a new problem. That's why it's important to know about the various lighting options available.

There are three basic types of artificial lighting: general, task, and accent. General lighting illuminates a large area—an overhead fixture is an example of this. Task lighting is designed to illuminate a specific area, such as a countertop used for food preparation. This can be an under-cabinet halogen light in the form of strips or "pucks." Another example of task lighting is the wall sconce on each side of the medicine cabinet in the top photo. Accent lighting can be anything from interior cabinet lights to pendants to wall sconces. In older homes, all the lighting typically came from a single overhead fixture, either incandescent or fluorescent. Modern homes still can use an overhead fixture, but these are rapidly being replaced by a combination of recessed lights, track lighting, and accent or decorative lighting.

Track lighting. Track lighting is a great way to provide customizable lighting in your home; individual lamps snap into a track anywhere along its length to spotlight different areas of the room or special wall treatments (middle photo). You can either replace an existing fixture with track lighting or have a new electrical box installed to add lighting to a new area in your home.

CHOOSING LIGHTBULBS

■ Halogen bulbs, very popular in recessed lights (or "cans"), show colors truer, but are pricier and not very energy-efficient. Also, they tend to throw off a lot more heat than other lighting types. Fluorescent lights don't heat up the surroundings and are more energy-efficient, but they do tend to make things (and people) look greenish; color-corrected versions are available for this reason. The old standby, incandescent light, is inexpensive, is energy-efficient, is available everywhere, and gives a warm glow. It's a good choice for vanity lighting. A new type of incandescent bulb manufactured by Verilux (www.verilux.net) creates a bright, white light similar to daylight—so similar, in fact, that the Natural Spectrum lightbulbs are marketed as "sunshine in a box." (Another new Verilux option: HappyEyes lamps, designed to increase contrast and reduce glare.)

Decorative or accent lighting. Decorative or accent lights come in a huge variety of styles and finishes, as shown in the top right photo. Wall sconces are commonly used as accent lights; just realize that these are to be used for setting a mood or highlighting an architectural feature and will need to be supplemented with general

lighting. Pendant lights are perfect for use around eating areas and work areas. There are two basic versions of a pendant light: one where the light is suspended simply by its electrical cord, or, like the ones shown in the photo above, where the light is suspended via a metal rod that hides the electrical cord.

RECESSED LIGHTING

■ If you decide to install recessed cans, keep things simple by buying a kit. Recessed lighting is widely marketed in separate components (trim, can, etc.), and it takes a pro to mix and match successfully. There are two other cautions about recessed lighting: The cans come in versions for new construction and for remodeling—make sure you buy the right type for your room. Remodeling lights attach to the ceiling via a set of clips; on new-construction lights, the light attaches to a pair of sliding brackets that are fastened to the ceiling joists.

It's also important to be careful about insulation: Buy recessed cans that are rated safe for contact with insulation; they'll be labeled "IC-rated," as illustrated in the bottom drawing. Otherwise, you'll have to move or remove ceiling insulation, and that can let energy go right up and out. And for the ultimate in flexibility, choose cans that have pivoting lenses so you can direct the light where you need it most.

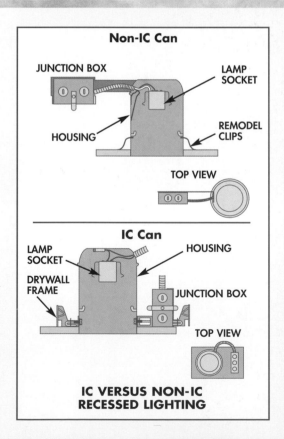

Non-IC Can

JUNCTION BOX
LAMP SOCKET
HOUSING
REMODEL CLIPS
TOP VIEW

IC Can

LAMP SOCKET
HOUSING
DRYWALL FRAME
JUNCTION BOX
TOP VIEW

IC VERSUS NON-IC RECESSED LIGHTING

3

ACCESSIBLE HOME SYSTEMS

A re you planning on doing your accessible home makeovers yourself or hiring out the work? Either way, you'll benefit by having a basic understanding of the different mechanical systems in your home that can be affected by a makeover. These include the electrical, plumbing, and framing systems. If you have a grasp of the fundamentals, you'll be better able to understand the work or the costs involved with something that may appear relatively simple, like moving a wall a few inches to widen a hallway. Although a few inches doesn't seem like much, electrical and/or plumbing lines in the walls will need to be re-routed, the ceiling and flooring will be disturbed, and ceiling or flooring joists may need to be strengthened. So, the more you know about these systems, the better prepared you'll be to do the work yourself, or budget for work and talk knowledgeably (and realistically) to contractors.

ACCESSIBLE KITCHEN & BATH

■ In terms of plumbing and electrical systems, the kitchen is the most complex room in your home, as illustrated in the drawing at right. Next in complexity is the bathroom; see the drawing on the opposite page. The systems in both rooms are similar in that they share the same components as described below. What varies from room to room is the complexity of the systems, which depends primarily on the number of fixtures and/or appliances in the room.

Plumbing system. Every kitchen or bathroom has three types of plumbing lines: supply, waste, and vent, as illustrated in the drawing at right and on the opposite page. Plumbing fixtures get pressurized water from the supply system; fresh water comes from either a local water utility or a private well. The pressure comes from the city's pumping stations or from the well pump, respectively. Water flows through a main shutoff valve and then to the hot-water heater. From there, hot and cold water branch out to different parts of the home. Solid and liquid waste is carried out of the home through the waste line. It uses gravity to move wastewater away from sinks, toilets, and tubs and into a line (often called the soil stack or main stack) that empties into the city sewer or a private septic tank. In between every fixture and the waste line is a trap that fills with enough water to create a seal that prevents sewer gas from entering the home. Vent lines allow wastewater in drain lines to flow freely. They also prevent water from being pulled out of the traps (siphoning), which would allow sewer gas into the home.

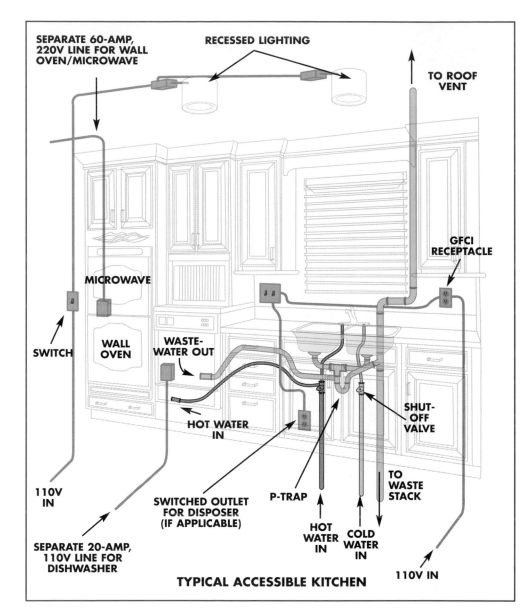

SEPARATE 60-AMP, 220V LINE FOR WALL OVEN/MICROWAVE

RECESSED LIGHTING

TO ROOF VENT

GFCI RECEPTACLE

MICROWAVE

SWITCH

WALL OVEN

WASTE-WATER OUT

HOT WATER IN

SHUT-OFF VALVE

110V IN

SWITCHED OUTLET FOR DISPOSER (IF APPLICABLE)

P-TRAP

TO WASTE STACK

SEPARATE 20-AMP, 110V LINE FOR DISHWASHER

HOT WATER IN

COLD WATER IN

110V IN

TYPICAL ACCESSIBLE KITCHEN

Electrical system. Electricity from the local utility connects to your home through the service head. It flows through the electric company's meter and then enters the house at the service panel. From the panel, electricity is distributed throughout the house and to the bathroom by individual circuits, each protected by either a fuse or a breaker. Individual circuits are connected to the service panel by a cable, or separate conductors protected by conduit. Current flows to a device through the "hot" or black wires, then returns to its source along the "neutral" or white wires. Control devices, like switches, are installed in the "hot" leg of the circuit. Kitchens usually require both 110- and 220-volt circuits—many of which are dedicated to a single appliance. Electric ranges, cooktops, and ovens require 110- and/or 220-volt receptacles. Some units use 220 for the burners or bake units and 110 for timer, clock, buzzer, and light. The 220-volt line for these is typically rated 40 to 60 amps. Dishwashers require a dedicated 110-volt, 20-amp line; garbage disposals usually don't require their own dedicated line. Most bathrooms usually need only 110-volt lines, but one or more may be dedicated to a single fixture, such as a jetted tub. Usually, 220-volt lines are needed only for electric heat, and occasionally for a heater built into a jetted tub or hot tub.

Dealing with code. It's important to know that you'll need a permit anytime you consider adding to or changing existing systems, running new systems, or upgrading substandard systems. Although this may seem a nuisance, building, electrical, and plumbing codes are written and enforced to protect you. Part of the confusion associated with many codes is that what is perfectly acceptable in one part of the country may be prohibited in another part. It's important to note that your local code supersedes the national code that it amends. The only way to make sure what applies to your home is to check the code at your local building department.

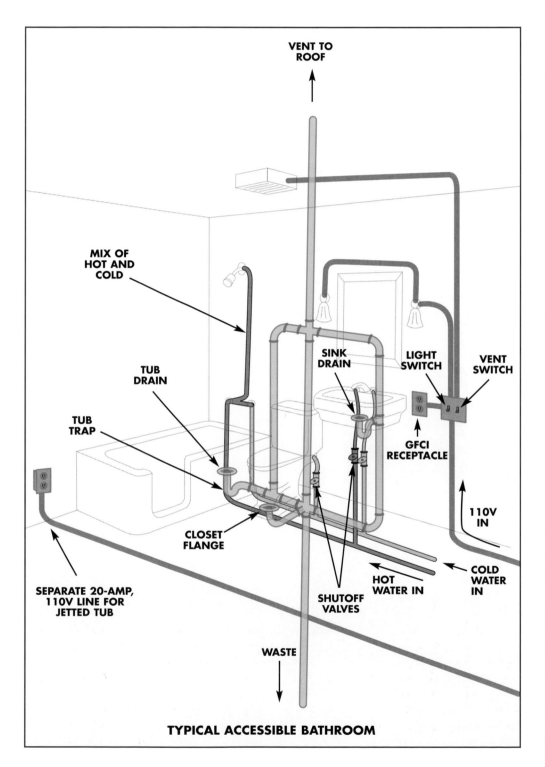

VENT TO ROOF

MIX OF HOT AND COLD

SINK DRAIN

LIGHT SWITCH

VENT SWITCH

TUB DRAIN

GFCI RECEPTACLE

TUB TRAP

110V IN

CLOSET FLANGE

COLD WATER IN

SEPARATE 20-AMP, 110V LINE FOR JETTED TUB

HOT WATER IN

SHUTOFF VALVES

WASTE

TYPICAL ACCESSIBLE BATHROOM

WALL FRAMING

In order to tackle some of the more challenging aspects of a makeover, such as moving walls or fixtures, you'll need a solid understanding of basic wall framing.

Wall types. There are two categories for the walls in a house: load-bearing and non-load-bearing. A load-bearing wall helps support the weight of a house; a non-load-bearing wall doesn't. All of the exterior walls that run perpendicular to the floor and ceiling joists in a structure are load-bearing walls because they support joists and rafters either at their ends or at their midspans, as illustrated in the drawing above. Any interior wall that supports the weight of the roof (like the center wall that sits directly below the center truss of the roof framing) is a load-bearing wall. Interior walls that sit above a girder or interior foundation wall are also load-bearing.

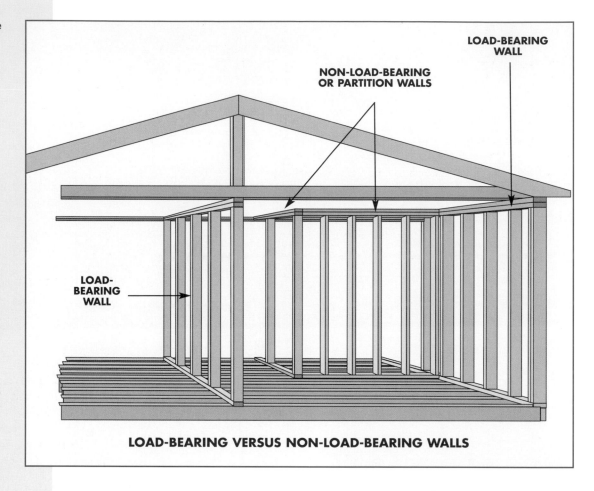

LOAD-BEARING VERSUS NON-LOAD-BEARING WALLS

Non-load-bearing walls, often called partition walls, have less rigid design rules and code requirements, such as wider stud spacing (24" vs. 16" on center) and smaller headers. This is because they don't support any of the structure's weight.

Wall framing. The standard in residential framing is a 2-by wall. It usually consists of vertical wall studs that run between the sole plate attached to the subfloor, and the top plate or double top plate, as illustrated in the top drawing on the opposite page. Anyplace a window or door requires an opening in the wall, a horizontal framing member called a header is installed to assume the load of the wall studs that were removed. The header is supported by jack studs (also called

trimmer studs) that are attached to full-length wall studs known as king studs. Cripple studs are the shorter studs that run between the header and the double top plate or from the underside of the rough sill of a window to the sole plate.

Framing and vent lines. Basic wall framing as described above is fairly straightforward. Things can get tricky, however, in bathrooms and kitchens when vent lines are involved, as these lines run inside the walls. This means that if you need to move a fixture or appliance, or are considering adding a window or flush-mount cabinet (like a medicine cabinet), you need to know where these lines are and how to modify them if need be.

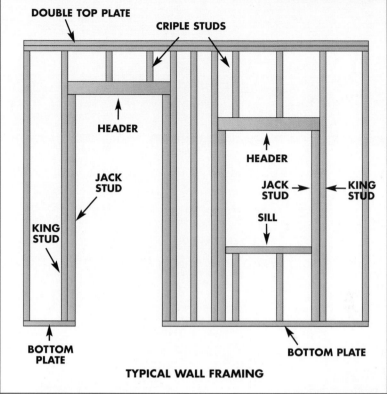

TYPICAL WALL FRAMING

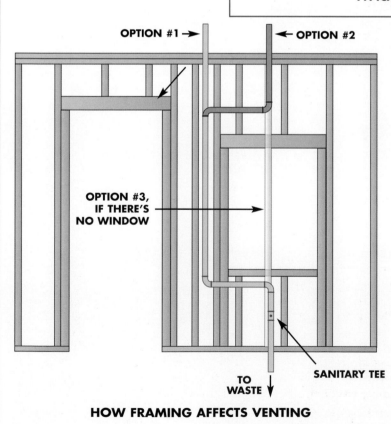

HOW FRAMING AFFECTS VENTING

Since most kitchens have windows directly above the sink, it's important to note that the vent line typically runs up and around the window, as illustrated in the bottom drawing. This is important if you're planning on moving or enlarging the window—the vent line may need to be re-routed, and you should consider the cost of this in your makeover budget. If you're considering adding a flush-mount medicine cabinet that is recessed into the wall as part of your makeover, you need to know that the vent line for most vanity sinks typically runs up through the wall directly behind the vanity sink (option #3 in the bottom drawing). So, you may need to re-rout the vent line.

How you frame an opening for a window or flush-mount cabinet will depend on whether the wall is load- or non-load-bearing (see page 56). Non-load-bearing walls will need just horizontal cleats to support the cabinet. On a load-bearing wall where studs are removed, though, openings require the addition of a header and cripple studs. These will take over the load-bearing work of the studs that were removed.

RAISED-HEIGHT APPLIANCES

If your accessible kitchen makeover plans call for raised-height appliances, you'll need to know what's involved with raising them. The two most commonly raised appliances in a kitchen are the dishwasher and wall oven. Both involve modifying your kitchen cabinets. This is tough to do on existing cabinets, but relatively easy when installing new cabinets.

Dishwasher. Since most dishwashers fit under the kitchen countertop, the first thing to realize is that you'll also need to raise the countertop when you raise the dishwasher, as illustrated in the bottom drawing. Because the countertop will need to be cut and the edges of the raised portion will be exposed, this technique works best with solid-surface materials, as shown in the top right photo. Raising the dishwasher is really just a matter of building a

sturdy platform for the dishwasher to sit on; the finished height of the platform is typically 9". This raises the dishwasher enough to greatly reduce bending and back fatigue. Plumbing lines will also need to be re-routed. For more on installing a raised-height dishwasher, see page 96.

Wall oven. Since wall ovens are usually installed in tall cabinets like the one shown in the middle photo, raising the oven requires modifying just the cabinet opening. Most cabinet manufacturers offer open-front cabinets designed expressly for this. The opening on virtually all of these cabinets will need to be adjusted to fit your specific wall oven. Typically, the opening is made oversized and you cut and attach filler strips to the sides as needed. In some cases, you may also need to cut the face of the cabinet to create an adequate opening. Then it's simply a matter of securing the wall oven to the cabinet. For more on installing a wall oven, see page 186.

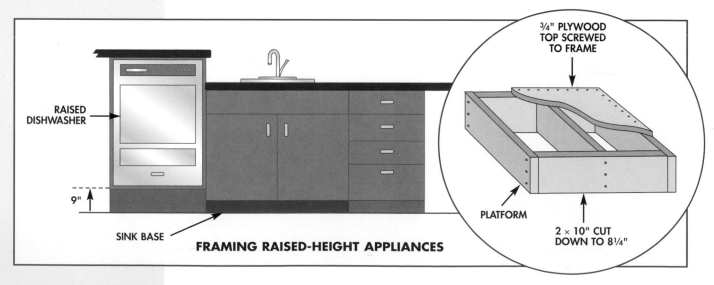

RAISED
DISHWASHER

9"

SINK BASE

FRAMING RAISED-HEIGHT APPLIANCES

¾" PLYWOOD
TOP SCREWED
TO FRAME

PLATFORM

2 × 10" CUT
DOWN TO 8¼"

FRAMING FOR SPECIALTY TOILETS

■ When your accessible bathroom makeover involves replacing an existing toilet with a specialty toilet—like a wall-hung toilet or in-wall tank toilet—you'll need to know how this affects wall framing. Note: Before you decide to purchase one of these units, verify the wall thickness behind the existing toilet. In many cases, a 2×6 stud wall is required; check the spec sheet on the toilet you're interested in before making a purchase to make sure it'll fit in your existing wall.

Framing a wall-hung toilet. Of the two specialty toilets, the wall-hung toilet is the simpler to frame. There are really two things that need to be modified. First, you'll need to firmly attach a horizontal cleat to the wall studs for mounting the toilet. This cleat is similar to that used for mounting a wall-hung sink, as described on page 60. The other modification involves the waste line. Since there's no base to a wall-hung toilet, you'll need to move the waste line into the wall and remove the existing closet bend and closet flange on the floor. This job is best left to a licensed plumber.

Framing an in-wall tank toilet. The ultimate space-saving toilet for a mature-friendly bathroom is the in-wall tank toilet shown in the top photo. The only portion of the toilet that protrudes into the room is the bowl itself; the flush activator is mounted on a nearby wall. Framing for one of these units can be complex, as illustrated by the drawings below and left. To fully support the tank and bowl, the wall behind the toilet will basically have to be reframed. Consult the installation instructions for the toilet you're interested in before starting work. As with a wall-hung toilet, you'll need to re-route the waste line and remove the old one.

Diagrams

- 5½"
- 2× 6 STUD WALL
- ½" SUPPLY
- FLUSH PLATE
- TANK
- 44½" – 48½"
- 22"
- WALL-MOUNTED TOILET
- 2" TRAP WAY
- FINISHED FLOOR
- 3"
- STUD FRONT CENTER HOLE

IN-WALL TANK: SIDE VIEW

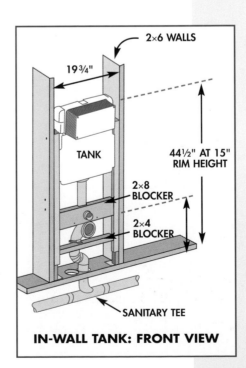

- 2×6 WALLS
- 19¾"
- TANK
- 44½" AT 15" RIM HEIGHT
- 2×8 BLOCKER
- 2×4 BLOCKER
- SANITARY TEE

IN-WALL TANK: FRONT VIEW

FRAMING FOR SPECIALTY SINKS

■ There are several space-saving and access-creating specialty sinks that can be installed in a mature-friendly bathroom: wall-mount sinks, pedestal sinks, and semi-mount sinks.

Wall-mount sinks. Wall-mount sinks are suspended from the wall or a bracket attached to the wall. This means the framing behind the wall covering must be strengthened to bear the weight of the sink. This usually entails adding a horizontal support cleat between nearby wall studs, as shown in the left photo and illustrated in the middle drawing.

Pedestal sinks. What many homeowners don't know is that a pedestal sink is actually a wall-mount sink. Yes, some weight is borne by the pedestal, but the main load is supported by the wall. If you're replacing a wall-mount sink (at roughly the same height) that was installed properly, you can use the same cleat and won't

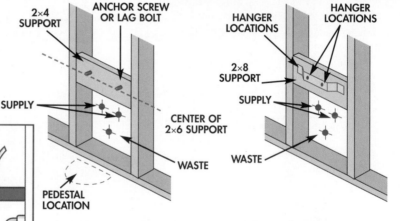

2×4 SUPPORT

ANCHOR SCREW OR LAG BOLT

HANGER LOCATIONS

HANGER LOCATIONS

2×8 SUPPORT

SUPPLY

SUPPLY

CENTER OF 2×6 SUPPORT

WASTE

WASTE

PEDESTAL LOCATION

PEDESTAL AND WALL-HUNG SINK FRAMING

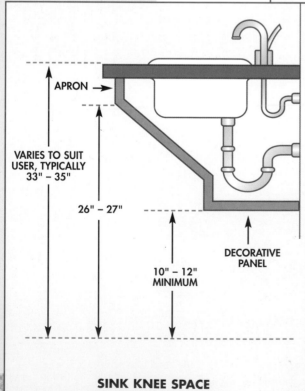

APRON

VARIES TO SUIT USER, TYPICALLY 33" – 35"

26" – 27"

DECORATIVE PANEL

10" – 12" MINIMUM

SINK KNEE SPACE

need to remove the wall covering. But, if you're replacing a vanity, you'll have to remove the wall covering and add the cleat. This is something to keep in mind when estimating time and costs.

Semi-mount sinks. Another type of bathroom sink that often requires modifying framing is the semi-mount sink, like the one we installed in the master bathroom makeover and shown on page 65. This specialty sink fits into a recess in a countertop that either attaches to the rear wall or attaches between a wall and a partition wall, or both. When framing for and installing this type of sink, it's important to be aware of recommended knee-space clearances, as illustrated in the bottom drawing.

For the real-life makeovers in this book, we tackled almost every room in a home that hunkered on the low end of ordinary. It's a 1980 ranch (single-level) with three bedrooms, two baths, and lots of access problems (not to mention cosmetic issues). A former rental property, this home challenged us at every turn: narrow hallways, limited bath access, slippery, cracked tile floors, a nightmare kitchen... this was the ugly duckling that we transformed into a swan (mature-friendly, of course).

Because of the enormity of this task, we switched from our standard makeover format of redoing a space three times at three spending levels: economy, mid-range, and high-end. To create our accessible home, we upgraded each of our target rooms once, to increase access, safety, and appeal. As with the other "MoneySmart Makeover" series books, we're not suggesting that you duplicate our makeovers. We urge you to choose the projects that fit best in your home, with your needs and budget.

Each of the makeovers includes photos of the subject rooms "before" and "after," and a list of projects we did for the makeover, along with approximate costs. Maybe you'll get a design idea here...knowledge of helpful new products there... some do-it-yourself technique tips here. There's room in every project for your personal tastes and preferences.

Once you "shop" these pages for ideas and real-world inspiration, move on to Part 3: Creating Your New Look.

KITCHEN MAKEOVER

ORIGINAL GUEST BATHROOM

The guest bath made one cringe at every turn, from the stained fiberglass tub/shower to the inaccessible sink to the cracked, slick tile floor. A standard-height toilet (missing its tank lid) and a narrow door opening completed the aging-unfriendly package. Also standard: an "access" hallway barely wide enough for a walker, let alone a wheelchair.

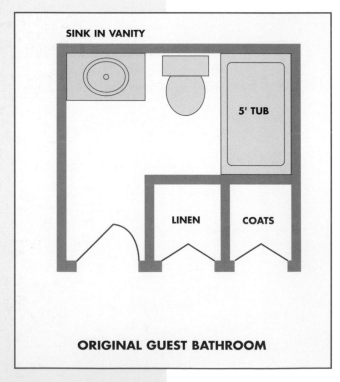

SINK IN VANITY

5' TUB

LINEN   COATS

ORIGINAL GUEST BATHROOM

GUEST BATHROOM MAKE

■ First we gutted the bathroom, then opened up the hallway wall as described in the hallway makeover on page 69. Out went the linen closet, replaced by corner shelving. By angling the door into the bathroom (and adjacent bedroom), we created a 60" turning radius for a wheelchair; the new door we installed was 36" wide. More major upgrades: a walk-in tub with shower surround and grab bars, raised-height toilet, wall-mount sink, and tileboard on the walls. Add in a textured tile floor, light, vent, and accessories, and you have a sleek new bath that anyone can happily use.

WHAT WE DID

Removed old fixtures and flooring ($0)
Modified hallway wall ($100)
Installed the following:
   Wall-mount sink ($375)
   Lever-style sink faucet ($150)
   Raised-height toilet ($525)
   Tileboard walls ($150)
   Grab bars ($150)
   Wall-mount accessories ($550)
   Mosaic tile floor ($200)
   Walk-in jetted bathtub ($2,500)
   Shower surround ($1,200)
   Lever-style tub/shower faucet ($300)
   Motion-activated light/vent ($400)
   Wall light ($50)
   Paddle-style electrical switches ($10)
Total cost: $5,200–$6,700, depending on materials selected

WALL-MOUNT SINK
RAISED-HEIGHT TOILET
WALK-IN TUB
BUILT-IN CORNER SHELVING
36" DOOR

GUEST BATHROOM MAKEOVER

ORIGINAL MASTER BATHROOM

While the cramped master bath looked slightly better than the guest bath, that's not saying much. A bulky vanity and narrow door limited access, while the smooth, worn tile floor invited accidents. The shower unit did have a seat, but its threshhold was high and showerhead fixed in place. One overhead fluorescent tube illuminated this drab muddle of a bathroom.

MASTER BATHROOM MAKEOVER

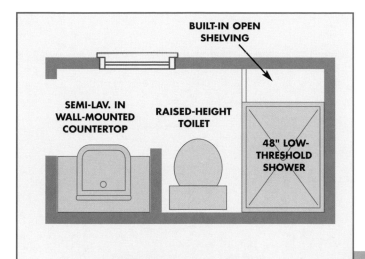

BUILT-IN OPEN SHELVING

SEMI-LAV. IN WALL-MOUNTED COUNTERTOP

RAISED-HEIGHT TOILET

48" LOW-THRESHOLD SHOWER

MASTER BATH MAKEOVER

■ After we gutted the whole room, the fun began. We removed the door wall to get the sleek, one-piece shower unit in, with its low threshold, adjustable handheld shower spray, ample seat, and grab bar. Open shelving replaced the old vanity storage, which itself made way for a fully accessible semi-mount sink. Storage was gained with a built-in medicine cabinet, flanked by wall sconce lighting. A raised-height toilet and wall heater add comfort and ease, while a neutral, textured tile makes the floor safer (and less prominent). Faux-painted walls and laminate countertop give a cool, blue imprint to this cool—and accessible—new space.

WHAT WE DID

Removed old fixtures and flooring ($0)
Installed the following:
  One-piece low-threshold shower ($700)
  Bypass shower door ($350)
  Adjustable showerhead and faucet ($200)
  Open shelving ($100)
  Ceramic tile flooring ($200)
  Raised-height toilet ($525)
  Partition wall for new sink ($50)
  New sink countertop ($100)
  Semi-mount sink ($225)
  Lever-style faucet ($200)
  Built-in medicine cabinet ($250)
  Lighting ($100)
  Motion-activated vent ($400)
  Wall heater ($250)
  Faux-finish walls ($50)
  Lever-style door handset ($25)
  Paddle-style electrical switches ($10)
Total cost: $3,000–$4,000, depending on materials selected

Original Living and Dining Room

Ripply, stained carpet in the living room and cracked tile in the dining area hid an uneven concrete subfloor. The tacky popcorn ceiling boasted two battered, semi-functioning fans, and cheap, unpainted wood trim stood out way too much. While the open plan allowed good access, these rooms begged for upgrades.

BACK PATIO

DINING AREA

LIVING ROOM

FRONT DOOR

LIVING AND DINING ROOM MAKEOVER

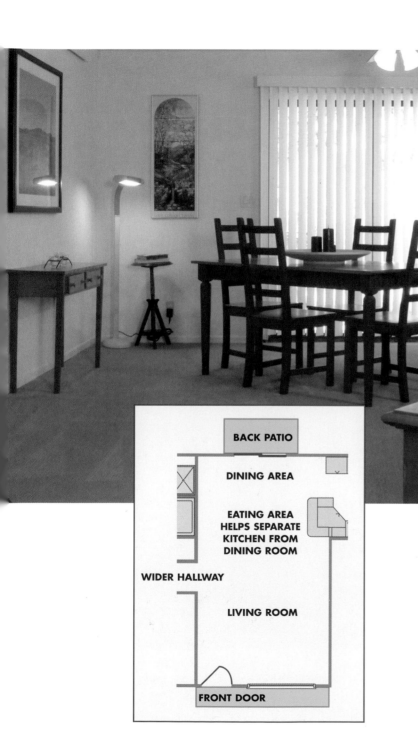

BACK PATIO

DINING AREA

EATING AREA HELPS SEPARATE KITCHEN FROM DINING ROOM

WIDER HALLWAY

LIVING ROOM

FRONT DOOR

■ This makeover might seem mostly cosmetic, but it features real aging-in-place improvements. We scraped off the popcorn ceiling, painted the walls and ceiling, and installed quiet, efficient ceiling fans (with remote controls) to help circulate air and cut energy costs. The old flooring—bad carpet, worse tile—was a hazard to feet of any age; ditto the uneven subfloor. After leveling the floor, we installed padding and a quality "resi-mercial" carpet of soft yet long-wearing nylon for the whole space. Its low nap accommodates feet, walkers, and wheelchairs easily. A high-tech "natural light" lamp now helps illuminate a homey, pleasant space that welcomes all.

WHAT WE DID

Removed old flooring ($0)

Replaced trim ($150)

Painted walls ($150)

Installed low-nap, close-weave carpeting ($1,800)

Installed two new ceiling fans ($450)

Installed paddle-style switches ($25)

Installed lever-style handset on front door ($75)

Added eating area per kitchen makeover (pages 70–72)

Total cost: $2,000–$3,000, depending on materials selected

ORIGINAL HALLWAY

For someone in a wheelchair, this hallway led nowhere. You couldn't fit, or access the bedrooms and baths that led off it: The doors were 30" wide or less, with no turning space. The same foot-catching carpet as in the living room covered more faulty subfloor. On the plus side, at least there were linen and storage closets.

30"
DOOR

30"
DOOR

LINEN

← 36" →

COATS

HALLWAY MAKEOVER

Nasty carpeting hit the trash to prep for the big work: bracing, then removing the wall to widen the hall-way (not a job for novices). We framed the new wall, adding wider, angled doorways for bedrooms and baths, plus a built-in storage unit of drawers and cupboards (simple stock cabinets screwed together and fastened to wall studs). With new dry-wall and paint, doors, and handsets, it was almost perfect. Finishing touches: a helpful handrail, plus low-nap, dense carpeting. Now this is a hallway that gets you somewhere.

WHAT WE DID

Removed old flooring ($0)
Removed one wall ($0)
Painted walls ($50)
Installed the following:
   New wall with angled doorways ($300)
   36"-wide doors – bathroom/bedroom ($350)
   Lever-style door handsets ($50)
   Built-in storage from stock cabinets ($250)
   Door and baseboard trim ($125)
   Low-nap, close-weave carpeting ($320)
Total cost: $1,000 –$2,100, depending on materials selected

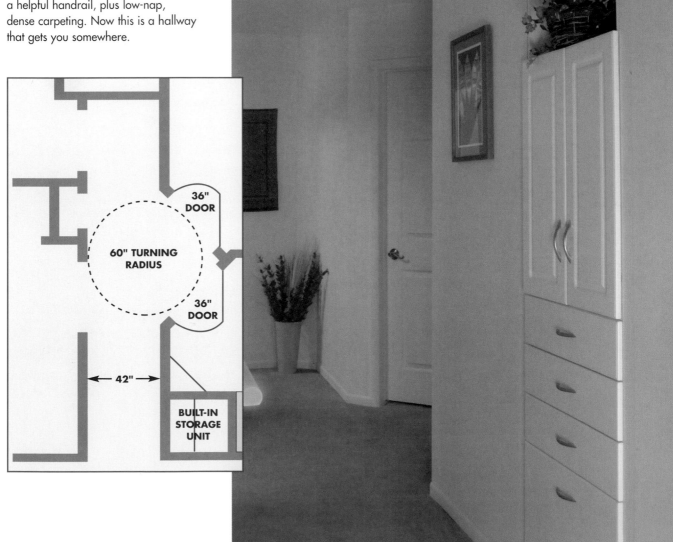

36" DOOR

60" TURNING RADIUS

36" DOOR

42"

BUILT-IN STORAGE UNIT

ORIGINAL KITCHEN

■ One word captures the "before" kitchen: demolition. The lowered ceiling and poor lighting gave it that dungeon feeling, accented by shabbily made, poorly designed, and poorly installed cabinets. Broken, slick tiles had overlain a cracked concrete subfloor. Bonus: a fine view of the hot water heater and laundry area. Yuck.

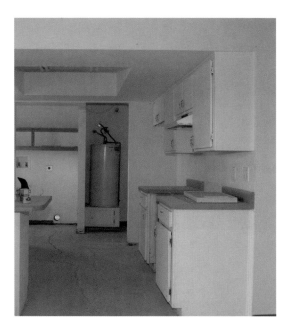

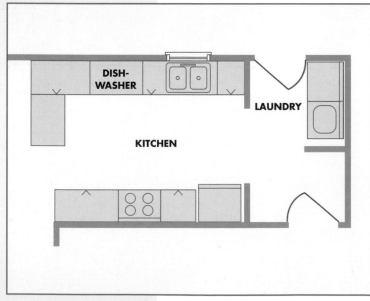

KITCHEN MAKEOVER

Honest, it's the same kitchen, revamped as a beautifully accessible room. Highlights: handsome Timberlake cabinets (those under the sink and cooktop were modified for wheelchair access), and extra storage under the wide-open peninsula breakfast bar. All hardware is easy-to-use pulls, and all appliance controls are front and center (combination wall oven/microwave, raised dishwasher, and cooktop). Aging eyes can readily distinguish the gorgeous teal, solid-surface countertop with its white edging; added visibility shines from recessed lighting in the raised ceiling and from directional lights over the sink. Textured ceramic floor tiles extend into the laundry area, now shielded by custom pocket doors with ready-made glass inserts. In all, a marvelously mature and accessible kitchen.

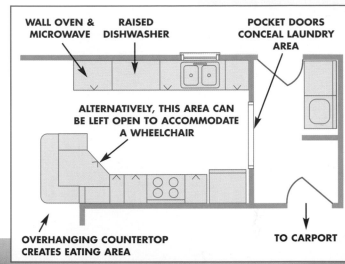

WALL OVEN & MICROWAVE

RAISED DISHWASHER

POCKET DOORS CONCEAL LAUNDRY AREA

ALTERNATIVELY, THIS AREA CAN BE LEFT OPEN TO ACCOMMODATE A WHEELCHAIR

OVERHANGING COUNTERTOP CREATES EATING AREA

TO CARPORT

WHAT WE DID

Removed flooring and cabinets ($0)

Removed perimeter soffit ($0)

Removed existing partition walls ($0)

Installed new ceiling ($200)

Recessed lighting ($100)

Ran electrical for new appliances ($200)

Framed new partition walls for pocket door ($100)

Installed drywall as needed ($150)

Painted walls ($100)

Installed the following:

  Ceramic tile floor ($400)

  New cabinets ($10,500)

  Solid-surface countertop ($4,000)

  Solid-surface sink ($500)

  Lever-style kitchen faucet ($150)

  Wall oven/microwave ($2,500)

  Raised dishwasher ($700)

  Cooktop ($900)

  New range hood ($200)

  Pocket doors ($400)

  Glass inserts in pocket doors ($400)

  Paddle-style switches ($25)

Total cost: $17,500–$22,500, depending on materials selected

Seemingly small details can have a big impact on the ease, convenience, and appeal of a cabinet...an appliance...indeed, a whole room. Here, some detailed insights into just a few features of our new, mature-friendly kitchen.

Built-in eating area. Call it a breakfast bar, call it a built-in eating area—whatever the case, you'll call this peninsula super-handy for its all-around access. Two important details: The solid-surface countertop is edged in white for high-contrast visibility, and it sits atop sturdy yet graceful supports that beautifully accent the cabinetry.

Separate cooktop. The controls for this elegant cook-top are at the front for easy, safe reach by users of (almost) all abilities. For wheelchair access, the cabinet under the cooktop can be modified (see page 97). Another great touch: The range hood by Broan features bright halogen lighting and will turn itself off automatically, too.

Before: This laundry room came complete with a cracked subfloor, virtually no storage, a companion hot water heater (for the aesthet-

ics, we guess, plus lack of other space), and as an extra feature, you could see the whole affair from the kitchen and dining room. Ease and appeal went right down the drain.

After: The pocket doors are much more than pretty: These custom-made extras with ready-made, translucent glass inserts make efficient use of the space, and at the same time separate the utility/laundry area from living areas. They open up to a new washer and dryer, both front-loading and with

up-front controls for access. Access is enhanced by the pedestals that raise the machines to a comfort-able height. And finally, who wouldn't love the unobtrusive cabinets with pull-down shelving (page 104) to bring items to eye level? All in all, washday struggles are rinsed away.

WHAT WE DID

Removed old storage rack ($0)

Painted walls ($25)

Installed stock storage cabinets ($200)

Tiled floor ($100)

Installed pull-down shelving racks ($500)

New front-load appliances ($900)

Installed pedestals ($200)

Installed paddle-style switches ($15)

Total cost:
$1,500–$2,000, depending on materials selected

Creating Your New Look

Ready to start your own mature- and accessible-friendly makeovers? Whether you'll tackle projects yourself or hire them out, this section will show you what's involved. With all the material covered so far about options, products, and prices under your (tool) belt, you're ready to get the inside story.

Using step-by-step photos and text, we'll show you how to do the projects detailed in these major categories: flooring, cabinets and countertops, walls, steps and hallways, windows and doors, plumbing, and electrical. Depending on your personal makeover needs and plans, maybe you'll try just one, two—or even all—of the projects covered.

The beginning of each category features an "after" photo to show the results of the tasks involved. And each project includes several in-process photos, plus a list of the tools you'll need, to help you every accessible step of the way.

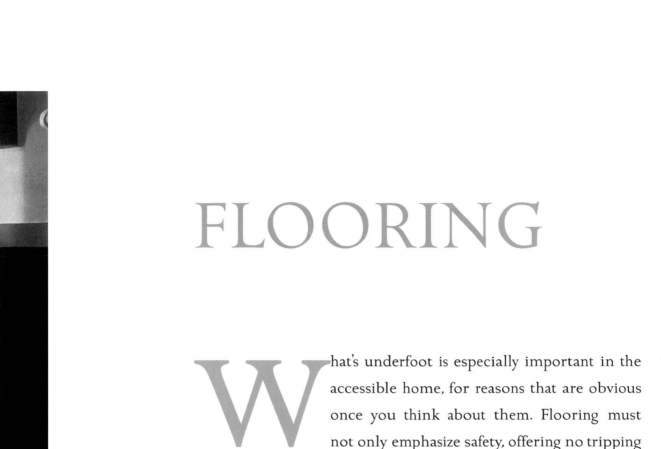

FLOORING

What's underfoot is especially important in the accessible home, for reasons that are obvious once you think about them. Flooring must not only emphasize safety, offering no tripping hazards, but it must also be easy to navigate when using a cane, walker, or wheelchair. That's why we recommend only three basic types of floor materials: ceramic tile, sheet vinyl, and low-pile, densely woven carpeting. In this chapter, we'll show you how to install all three. We'll also show you how to handle the all-important flooring transitions from room to room—any of which, done improperly, can create a tripping hazard.

Whatever the size or complexity of the area involved, it's important to have a rough plan of the room so that a flooring supplier can help you determine the correct amount of flooring to order. You don't need a work of art—just a rough sketch, including accurate dimensions and door openings.

Ceramic Tile

TOOLS

- Electric drill
- Putty knife
- Notched trowel
- Rubber-faced or dead-blow mallet
- Tile cutter and nipper
- Grout float
- Bucket and sponge
- Foam brush

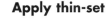

With one condition, ceramic floor tile is great for the accessible home: As long as you select a non-slip, textured tile (nothing glassy or mirror-smooth) and install it correctly (or have it done by a pro), you'll have a durable, easy-movement floor. While ceramic tile is do-it-yourself friendly, there are two issues to keep in mind. First, ceramic tile requires special tools to cut and install it (see the list above and the sidebar on page 78). And, it also takes longer to install than other flooring, mainly because you have to wait for materials to set up, like the mortar that holds the tile to the floor and the grout that fills the gaps between tiles. But if you break each of the tasks into separate steps, it's really very simple.

what will look best is to lay a row or two of tiles on the floor, as shown in the bottom left photo. Try a square pattern, or possibly one where the tiles are oriented diagonally to the corners of the room. Remember to leave a space between the tiles roughly equivalent to the size of the grout joint that you've chosen. Better yet, insert tile spacers between the tiles as you lay them down. When you've identified the pattern, snap a chalk line to establish a starting point for the tile (top right photo).

Establish a layout. The first step in laying ceramic tile is to establish the pattern you want. The best way to visualize

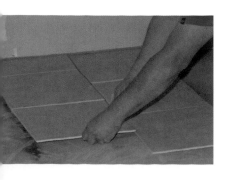

Apply thin-set mortar. Mix up enough thin-set mortar to cover about 4 square feet. Then use a square-notched trowel to spread the mortar on the floor or cement board, as shown in the bottom right photo. Most thin-set mortar manufacturers suggest a $1/4$" notch for tiles 12" or less in length; larger tiles may require a $1/2$" notch.

Set the full tiles. Start by setting a full tile along your reference chalk line. Press down as you lay the tile to force it into the mortar, as shown in the middle left photo. As soon as the tile is down, "set" it in the mortar by tapping it with a soft rubber-faced mallet; this makes the mortar spread evenly to give the best grip possible. Continue laying tiles along the reference line. To ensure consistent spacing, insert cross-shaped plastic tile spacers between each tile.

Level the tiles as you go. Even if you've leveled your floor (see the sidebar below), you'll often come across a tile that doesn't sit level on the floor. In situations like these, apply a dollop or two of thin-set mortar to the low areas, as shown in the top right photo. Replace the tile and check for level; add or remove mortar as needed.

LEVELING A FLOOR

■ Because they're brittle, ceramic tiles need a level underlayment that won't flex. The underlayment also must be impervious to moisture. The solution is cement board. It comes in $1/4$"- or $1/2$"-thick sheets. Attach cement board to an existing wood subfloor with thin-set mortar and screws. Secure it every 6" along the edges and every 8" throughout the interior. Then apply mesh tape over the seams and spread a layer of mortar over the tape with a putty knife. If you're installing tile on a concrete floor, it may need to be leveled, as shown at right.

Apply leveler. Professional flooring contractors have a number of leveling compounds available. Self-leveling compound is expensive, but easy to work with: You mix up a batch and pour it on the floor; as it spreads, it self-levels. But self-levelers have to dry overnight, so most pros use a quick-drying compound that they mix up with a dry powder and a liquid catalyst. These compounds "cure" by chemical reaction and set up quickly, as shown in the photo above.

Sand smooth. Regardless of the leveling compound, most surfaces will need to be smoothed before thin-set mortar is applied. Pros use a special abrasive tool like the one shown in the photo above to scrub the surface smooth.

Install partial tiles. Partial tiles are installed once the full tiles have been laid and set (top left photo). A partial tile is any tile that's not a full tile and has been cut to fit around an outside corner or other obstacle, such as a closet flange. To create a partial tile, you first mark it as follows: Place a tile on the nearest full tile to the wall. Then set a 1/8" spacer against the wall and place a "marker" tile on top of the tile to be cut, as illustrated in the drawing at right. Slide the marker tile until it butts against the spacer. Next, draw a line on the tile, using the edge of the marker tile as a guide. Now you can get an accurate fit when you cut the bottom tile. Once all the tiles are in place, let the mortar set up overnight.

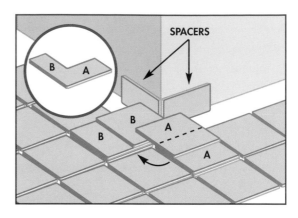

Apply grout. Before you apply grout, remove any plastic spacers. Mix up only enough grout to work a small section of tile at a time. This not only allows you to take your time to do the job right, but it also makes mixing easier, since you're working with smaller batches. Start in a corner and pour some grout on the tile. Use a grout float to force the grout into the joints, as shown in the middle photo.

CUTTING CERAMIC TILE

■ What type of tile are you using? What obstacles do you need to navigate? These answers will determine the type of cutting tools you'll need. The two main tile-cutting tools are the tile cutter and the motorized tile saw. (Note: For odd-shaped tiles, you can cut tiles with a rod saw, or remove small bits with a tile nipper.)

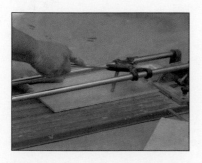

Tile cutter. It's easy to cut and snap straight lines on thin, relatively smooth tiles with a tile cutter. Just insert the tile into the cutter and align the cutting wheel with your marked line. Then draw the cutting wheel across the tile surface to score it. To snap the tile at the scored line, simply press the cutter handle down firmly.

Motorized tile saw. If you have a lot of tile to cut, consider renting a motorized tile saw; it cuts quantities of tile, and thick or rough textures, easily. These saws use diamond-impregnated blades, as well as water to keep the blade cool and to wash away the slurry created from cutting the tile.

Remove any excess grout.
Once you've applied the grout and forced it into the gaps between the tiles, hold the float at an angle to skim off the excess, as shown in the top left photo. Take care not to overwork the grout; as it dries, it's easier to inadvertently pull out the grout from between the tiles.

Clean and seal the tile. Although removing the remaining grout from the tiles with a sponge is straightforward, it takes time. Have a large bucket of water on hand and refill it with clean water often. Just as you did with the float, wipe the sponge diagonally over the tiles (middle photo above). Wipe each grout joint only once; repeated wiping can pull the grout out of the joint. After the grout has dried, use a soft cloth to wipe away any haze. Finally, since grout is porous, it needs to be sealed to prevent staining. To prevent the sealant from trapping moisture in, wait two to four weeks before applying a sealant to the grout joints only. Wipe up any excess sealer with a clean, dry rag.

MOSAIC TILE

■ Mosaic tile isn't a pattern, it's a size—any tile 2" square or smaller. Most mosaic tiles are mounted on a backing sheet of rubber, plastic, or heavy thread that groups the tiles in sections for easier installation. You don't have to be concerned with tile spacing, since it's already preset. All you have to take care of is the spacing between the tile sheets. You'll find mosaic tiles in 12"-square sheets and other sheet dimensions, depending on the design.

Establish the pattern.
Take the time to make a dry test of the pattern. Lay sheets of mosaic tile in place and check to see how they butt up against walls. To prevent narrow tiles at the walls, offset the tiles so there are equal partial tiles on both walls.

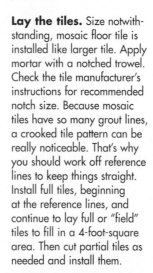

Lay the tiles. Size notwithstanding, mosaic floor tile is installed like larger tile. Apply mortar with a notched trowel. Check the tile manufacturer's instructions for recommended notch size. Because mosaic tiles have so many grout lines, a crooked tile pattern can be really noticeable. That's why you should work off reference lines to keep things straight. Install full tiles, beginning at the reference lines, and continue to lay full or "field" tiles to fill in a 4-foot-square area. Then cut partial tiles as needed and install them.

Apply the grout. There's a lot more grout involved in grouting mosaic tile than with standard tile. That's really the only difference of any note. Apply the grout with a float, pushing the grout into the gaps between the tiles. Then hold the float at an angle and squeegee off the excess. Use a damp sponge to clean the tile. When the tile is dry, wipe off the haze with a clean cloth. Wait two to four weeks for the grout to dry before you apply grout sealer.

Installing Sheet Vinyl

TOOLS

- Electric drill
- Utility knife
- Level and tape measure
- Trowel
- Framing square and straightedge
- Flooring roller

Sheet vinyl flooring is a good choice for the accessible home—as long as it's the non-slip, textured variety. Sheet vinyl is inexpensive, durable, and easy to install, and it comes in many patterns and colors. And, most quality vinyl flooring comes with a built-in cushion to make it easy on your feet. There are two ways to install sheet vinyl: full-adhesive and perimeter-install. Sheet vinyl flooring that's attached to the entire subfloor with adhesive is referred to as a full-adhesive installation. Since the flooring is firmly glued in place, it's very durable. This is especially true if it's a single piece; without seams, water, dirt, and dust can't sneak under it to weaken the glue bond—which is why we chose this type of install for the entryway shown here.

On a perimeter-install, the flooring is attached only around the perimeter with staples. The rest of the flooring "floats" on the subfloor. The advantage to this is it's not as messy as a full-adhesive installation. The disadvantage? Since most of the flooring isn't attached, it can tear or rip easily—even high-heeled shoes can damage it. Also, since most perimeter-installed sheet vinyl is stretched slightly as it's attached, any sharp object that's dropped can easily puncture the flooring, often creating a large rip.

Use a template. Since sheet vinyl goes down in one piece, there's little margin for error. The best way to prevent mistakes is to make a template of the floor and use it to cut the flooring. Start by butting a roll of heavy paper into a corner of the room. Temporarily fasten the template to the floor by cutting small triangles in the paper near the edges, and pressing strips of tape over each hole (middle photo).

If necessary, overlap large pieces 2", and fasten them at the seams; cut the template to match the perimeter as needed. When done, remove the template and place it on the sheet vinyl, adjusting its position so it's centered on the pattern and so the pattern is as close to equal as possible on all sides (bottom right photo).

Cut the sheet vinyl. Once the template is fastened down, cut the flooring to match the template. Using a utility knife, start by making the straight perimeter cuts, using a metal straightedge as a guide (top photo). Slide a scrap of plywood underneath to protect the floor. Then make any curved or obstacle cuts. For intricate curves, make a series of light cuts instead of one heavy one.

Test the fit. Before you break out the adhesive, it's best to test the fit of your flooring, as shown in the photo at left. If your template was accurate and you cut with precision, the piece should fit perfectly. Slide the flooring in place and check the fit around its perimeter.

Apply the adhesive. If you're working with a large piece of sheet vinyl, pull one side back toward the center and apply flooring adhesive with the recommended trowel. Then unfold it back into position. Repeat this process for the other half. If you're working with a small piece, simply remove it and apply the adhesive, as shown in the photo at right. With large or multiple pieces, it's best to roll and press one piece in place at a time (see below). This gives the other piece a solid edge to butt up against—there's just a lot less slipping and sliding around this way.

Press the sheet in place. The final, very important step is to firmly press the flooring in place to get a good bond. A rental tool called a flooring roller is used for this; if you skip this, you'll likely be plagued with air bubbles and loose sections. A 75- or 100-pound roller rents for less than $20 a day in most areas. Begin rolling in the center of the room, working your way toward the wall. This pushes out air bubbles so they can escape, and moves any excess adhesive to the edges, where it can be removed. On small areas like the one shown here, you can use a laminate roller or rolling pin to press the sheet vinyl firmly into the adhesive. Clean up any adhesive squeeze-out with a clean rag.

Carpeting

TOOLS

- Hammer and pry bar
- Staple gun
- Carpet or utility knife
- Seaming iron (rental)
- Metal snips
- Carpet stretcher (rental)
- Knee kicker (rental)
- Chalk line
- Stair tool
- Carpet edge trimmer (optional)

Soft, insulating, and noise-reducing, carpet by its very cushioning nature can help lessen the effect of a fall. And by choosing mature-friendly carpeting, you can have all these advantages, plus safety and durability. The good news is that you can take advantage of the hundreds of different carpet types, fibers, patterns, and colors available almost everywhere—just be sure to choose quality. What you're after is a low-pile (or low-nap), dense carpet that won't trip or snag aging feet, canes, or walkers, and that won't bog down a wheelchair.

Our choice was a go-with-everything carpet made of Honeywell Anso nylon, from Blueridge Home (www.ansonylon.com; www.blueridgecarpet.com). Both soft and tough, Anso Caress offers easy care and a silky "feel," plus outstanding durability. This carpet is low-pile and extremely dense, with slight texturing for visual interest. (Note: Honeywell Nylon and Blueridge are at the forefront of a trend called "resi-mercial"—carpet that merges the dense, low-pile durability of commercial products with the soft feel of residential carpet.)

Once you've selected carpet, it's important to recognize up front that installation is not for beginners. Special tools are required and, for the most part, carpet is a relatively uncooperative material. For your first carpeting project, consider only a small square or rectangular room. Leave the larger rooms for later, or call in a professional.

Install the tackless strips. Carpet is stretched and held in place by hooking the underside of the carpet onto tackless strips secured to the subfloor around the perimeter of the room. With the angled pins of the strip pointing toward the wall, begin by nailing a strip to the floor in one corner of the room (bottom photo). Maintain a consistent gap between the wall and strip with scrap-wood spacers—check the installation instructions or contact a flooring contractor for the correct gap.

Install the pad. With the tackless strips in place, you can install the pad (consult a professional about which type is best for your carpet). Carpet padding often has a slick side and a rough side; always install it with the slick side up to make it easy to slide the carpet around during installation. If your padding is wide enough to cover the entire room, roll out enough to cover the floor. Work slowly and try not to pull the padding excessively. If it catches on something, stop and lift it off—don't pull—carpet padding has very little resistance to tearing. Position the padding in a corner and check to make sure it butts up against the tackless strips as shown in the top left photo. You can join pieces of padding together at the seams with tape as shown in the top left inset photo.

Roll out the carpet. With the padding in place, you can install the carpet. In most cases, a roll of carpet is both heavy and cumbersome. Enlist the aid of a helper to bring it into the room and help you unroll it. Start by positioning the roll along one wall, leaving about 6" of excess to run up the wall. Then carefully roll the carpet out until you hit the opposite wall, as shown in the bottom left photo.

Cut the carpet to fit. Where the roll butts up against the opposite wall, mark the back of the carpet at each edge. Then measure up about 3" and make another mark. Pull the carpet away from the wall and snap a chalk line to connect the marks. Cut along this line, using a sharp utility knife or a carpet knife. Make sure to insert a scrap of plywood or other protective material under the folded-back carpet before cutting. Alternatively, if you've got a good eye, you can slice though the front of the carpet with a carpet knife, as shown in the top right photo.

Relieve the corners. With the carpet cut to rough length, the next step is to slide it over so the long edge extends up the wall. To do this, straddle the carpet and pull it

until it runs up the wall about 3". You'll notice immediately that the carpet doesn't want to cooperate at the corners, as shown in the bottom right photo. Use a carpet or utility knife to relieve the buckling by slitting the carpet in the corners. Cut just the couple of inches necessary to get the carpet to nestle into the corner; don't cut too far—you'll fit these corners later after stretching the carpet.

SEAMING CARPET

■ Cutting and seaming carpet has a well-deserved reputation for being a bit nerve-wracking, for several reasons. First, quality carpet is an investment, and a mis-cut can be costly. Second, proper seaming technique requires the use of a hot-glue seaming iron. Since the iron melts the glue just long enough for you to join the pieces together, you must work quickly and without hesitation.

Cut the seam. If you need to join pieces of carpet, start by positioning two pieces so they overlap, as shown in the top photo. Be sure to include an extra 3" at each wall and 3 extra inches for the seam. Then use a carpet knife to cut first one seam, then the other.

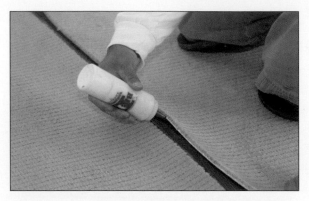

Treat the cut ends. The edges of most cut carpet will unravel over time. To prevent this, apply a bead of seam sealer along the cut edges of both seams, as shown in the photo above. Allow the glue to dry before proceeding.

Apply the seam tape. At this point you're ready to join the pieces of carpet. Although you can try gluing the carpet to the floor at the seams, a better method is to use hot-glue seam tape. You can find this wherever carpet is sold. The glue on the tape is melted with a special seaming iron available at most rental stores. Measure and cut a piece of tape to length and position it under the seam with the adhesive facing up. Next, slide a protective scrap of plywood under the seam tape. Place the iron under the seam directly onto the tape and plywood. In about 20 to 30 seconds, the glue will melt and you can slowly slide the iron along the tape. As you move the iron, let the carpet halves fall onto the hot glue. Work slowly in roughly 12" sections. Don't get nervous here: The iron won't burn the carpet or the glue, though both will get hot.

Press for a good bond. Every foot or so, stop sliding the seaming iron and press the edges of the carpet pieces down into the seam tape with your hands while squeezing the cut edges together. Even better: Use a small roller to press the carpet into the hot glue, as shown in the photo above. Continue like this until you're close to the seaming iron. Then repeat this process until the entire seam is complete.

arrows designate the knee kicker, while the longer arrows and the arrows that go from wall to wall call for the power stretcher. Between the weight of the power stretcher and the stiffness of the carpet, it's a good idea to enlist the aid of at least one helper for this demanding job.

To use a power stretcher, begin by placing the power head approximately 4" from the starting wall. Then attach extension tubes so the head reaches the opposite wall (top photo). At the opposite wall, attach the tail block where the carpet is already secured. Some tail blocks have wheels to make it easier to slide the stretcher along the wall. How much you need to stretch the carpet depends on the type, and whether you're stretching across its width or along its length. Ask for guidelines where you purchased your carpet.

Stretch the carpet. Carpet is stretched with two specialized tools—a knee kicker and a power stretcher—before it's secured to the tackless strips on the floor. Both are heavy-duty, professional-quality tools and are expensive. Fortunately, both can be found at a local rental center for around $100 a day. The power stretcher is the main tool that's used to stretch the carpet across the length and width of the room. The less-powerful but more agile knee kicker works best for securing the carpet in corners and around obstacles.

Just as important as the tools is the sequence that you use to stretch the carpet. The sequence illustrated below gives you the general idea. Short

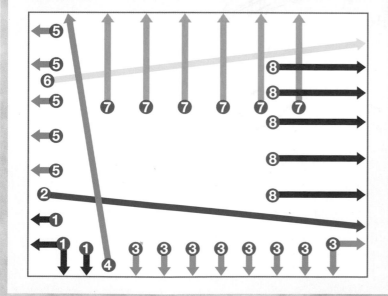

CARPET-STRETCHING SEQUENCE

Secure to tackless strips. Start by positioning the knee kicker about 3" to 5" inches away from the wall. This way you won't accidentally break one of the tackless strips loose. Holding the knee kicker securely with one hand, strike the pad sharply with your knee to stretch the carpet toward the wall. You may find it'll take a couple of whacks to fully stretch the carpet. Once in place, press the carpet firmly down onto the pins of the tackless strips, as shown in the middle right photo.

Tuck at strips. Once all the carpet edges have been cut, work your way around the room, tucking the edges of the carpet into the gap between the tackless strips and the wall. You can do this with a wide-blade putty knife or a special kind of chisel called a stair tool, as shown in the middle photo. Depending on the stiffness of the carpet, you may or may not need to use a hammer on the knife or chisel to persuade the carpet edge to cooperate.

Trim at walls. In a pinch, you can use a carpet knife or sharp utility knife to trim surplus carpet from the edges of the walls. The best tool for the job, however, is a carpet edge trimmer like the one shown in the top photo. You can rent one of these from your local rental store or purchase one from some home centers and most flooring suppliers. To use a carpet edge trimmer, hold it flat on the carpet and press it firmly into the wall as you move it slowly along the wall. Since it can't quite make it into corners, you'll need to complete the cut with a utility or carpet knife.

HEPA VACUUMS

■ To care for the carpeted and other surfaces in your home, consider vacuum cleaners that offer HEPA filters. This now-common acronym stands for High-Efficiency Particulate Arrestant—it means the filter is designed to capture dust, pet dander, and other allergens. How well a HEPA filter works can depend on the design of the vacuum cleaner itself. Miele, the appliance firm, offers a new line of vacuum cleaners featuring HEPA filters and super-efficient dustbags, plus a charcoal filter to absorb odors. The ART by Miele models (photo at left) are also lightweight yet powerful (1,000 watts), and are highly maneuverable. The telescopic handle adjusts, so it offers excellent usability for almost anyone.

Carpeting a Hallway

Carpeting a hallway is similar to carpeting a room, but with two differences. First, since most hallways are narrow, it's more challenging to fully stretch the carpet. Second, since hallways connect to other rooms, you're faced with how to handle the different transitions from the hallway flooring to the flooring used in the adjoining rooms; see the sidebar on page 89 for ways to handle transitions.

Install tackless strips. Position and nail tackless strips to the floor along the hallways as you would when carpeting a room (page 82). If you encounter an obstacle, such as a radiator, threshold, built-in, or door molding, cut the strips as needed into short lengths so you can work around the obstacle. Try to maintain the same gap that you used for the previous strips, and nail the cut strips to the floor as shown in the middle photo. Since tackless strips have angled pins protruding from one face and nails for securing the strips to the floor protruding from the other, they are a challenge to cut. The best way we've found to handle this is to cut them with metal snips—just make sure to wear leather gloves whenever handling these spiky strips.

Level as needed. Since the type of flooring can vary widely from hallway to room, you may be faced with different floor levels. Say, for example, the hallway is carpet but one of the bedrooms has a laminate floor over old vinyl tile. Depending on the flooring, this can easily be a difference of anywhere from $1/4$" to $3/4$". In situations like this, it's really important to create a gradual slope from one flooring to the other. This can be done by applying leveling compound to the subfloor to create a smooth, gradual slope, as shown in the bottom photo.

Install the pad. With the tackless strips in place and any leveling complete, you can roll out and cut the padding to fit, as shown in the top photo. Here again, cut it so it butts up to the tackless strips as closely as possible. On wood subfloors, it's a good idea to secure the padding to the subfloor with staples to keep it from shifting or bunching up; this is particularly important at high-traffic points, such as the thresholds of doors.

Position and cut the carpet. Since hallways are narrow, you'll need to pre-cut an oversized piece to fit from the main carpet roll. Measure the hallway and add 6" to both dimensions; cut a rough piece to size. This allows for a 3" excess at each wall. Relieve the corners as necessary, as shown in the middle photo.

Stretch the carpet. Before you stretch the carpet, you'll need to first handle any transitions (see page 89). Once all the transitions and seams are done, stretch the carpet. Start by stretching the length of the carpet with a power stretcher, as shown in the bottom photo. Then go back with a knee kicker and stretch the width of the hallway. Cut the carpet at the walls with a carpet knife and tuck the ends in between the tackless strips and the gap at the wall.

CARPET TRANSITIONS

■ There are three basic ways to handle carpet transitions: seam tape, adhesive, or metal transition strips; see the drawing below.

Seam tape. Carpet-to-carpet transitions are generally handled with hot-glue seam tape (bottom left photo). The procedure is similar to that used to seam together pieces of carpet when carpeting a room, as described on page 84. One challenge that may occur is if the carpets to be joined are of different thicknesses. In the mature home, even a slight shift in carpet height like this can create a tripping hazard. If this is the case, take the time to apply leveling compound under the thinner carpet to bring it up to the same level as the thicker carpet (as described at the bottom of page 87).

Adhesive. When carpeting has to transition to ceramic tile, the carpet is glued to the subfloor, where it butts up against the tile (bottom right photo). As with any seam, first seal the cut edges of the carpet to prevent it from unraveling over time before gluing it to the subfloor.

Transition strips. Metal transition strips are designed to handle the transition from carpeting to other flooring like sheet vinyl or ceramic tile. These metal strips attach to the subfloor with nails, screws, and/or glue. On some strips, one or both edges have C-shaped flanges. With these strips, you insert the flooring into the flange and then tap the top of the "C" to close the flange and tightly grip the flooring. Although these strips work well, they can create tripping hazards if care isn't taken to first bring both types of flooring up to the same level. If this isn't possible, you can find special transition strips called "reducers" at most hardware stores and home centers; see the bottom illustration in the drawing at right.

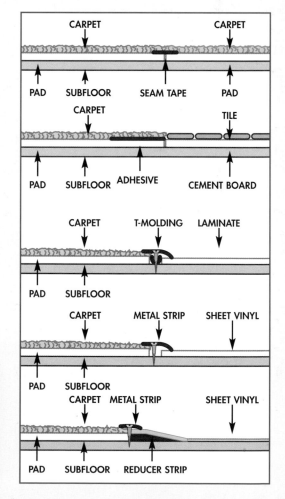

5

CABINETS & COUNTERTOPS

What makes a kitchen mature-friendly? Accessibility. That means many things: choosing appliances with front controls and raising up the dishwasher for easy reach, for example (see Chapter 2). It also means installing cabinets and countertops that can be accessed by someone either sitting or standing. With cabinets, this means sink and cooktop bases that are recessed, plus cabinet accessories like pull-out bins and pull-down shelving that make the contents just as accessible as the cabinets. With countertops, multiple levels (like those shown in the photo on the opposite page) are the answer to serving cooks at all levels.

In this chapter, we'll show you how to remove old cabinets, install new ones, and accessorize them. We'll also look at ways to modify existing cabinets to make them more accessible. Then we'll show you how solid-surface countertops are installed, and finish with an easy-to-build open shelving unit that provides instant access to its contents.

Demolition

TOOLS

- Pry bar and putty knife
- Screwdriver
- Drill with driver bit
- Adjustable wrench (optional)

To someone who's never ripped out a set of cabinets, it might seem like a simple job. You just pry them off the wall, right? Wrong. That's the last thing you want to do, because cabinets are screwed to the wall studs. To properly remove cabinets, you have to reverse-engineer the installation process. That is, you need to know how they were installed—check out pages 94–95 for base cabinet installation and pages 98–100 for wall cabinet installation.

Remove doors and drawers. To make it easier to remove and carry the cabinets, take the time to remove all the doors and drawers to lighten the load (bottom left photo). If you'll be reusing the cabinets for storage somewhere else (they make great shop cabinets), label the parts with masking tape before you remove them so you can reassemble them easily later.

Remove trim. Since the cabinet trim was the last thing installed, it's the first thing to go

in demolition. Use a pry bar as shown in the top right photo and remove all trim, including backsplashes.

Remove any cabinet attachments. Next you'll want to remove anything that's attached to the cabinets, like the range hood shown in the bottom right photo. With electrical units like this, first turn off and secure the power. Then remove the access panel and disconnect the wiring. Unscrew the mounting fasteners and carefully slide the unit out, taking care not to snag the electrical cable.

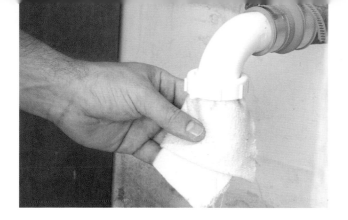

Check plumbing and electrical. Before you can remove the base units, you may need to disconnect plumbing lines; it all depends on how they were routed through the cabinet. If necessary, shut off the water and remove the shutoff valves if the piping comes up through the base of the cabinet. This will let you lift the cabinet up and out. Waste lines will need to be disconnected and temporarily plugged with a rag to prevent sewer gas from leaking into your house, as shown in the top photo.

Release and remove the cabinets. Most people find it easiest to first remove the base cabinets, then the wall cabinets. Doing so lets you get under the wall cabinets to support them as they're  removed from the wall. Since the countertop has to go eventually, disconnect the sink and faucet now and remove all the countertop fasteners. Then lift off the countertop and set it aside for reuse or disposal. This sequence gives you optimum access to the backs of the base cabinets where they're secured to the wall studs.

Depending on how the base cabinets were installed, you may have to remove the cove base or base trim. This is necessary only if you need to expose screws driven through the base of the cabinet into the floor to secure it. Otherwise, locate and remove the screws in the backs of the cabinets that secure them to the wall. You should now be able to lift and pull the base cabinets away from the wall as shown in the bottom left photo. If you encounter resistance, you may have missed a screw; locate and remove the screw or screws and try again. In older cabinets, these may be hard to find, as installers often covered screws with putty to hide them.

The wall units can now be removed. With a couple of helpers supporting each end of the wall cabinet, locate and remove the screws in the back of the cabinet that secure it to the wall. Lift the cabinet off the wall and set it aside. Repeat for the remaining wall units.

DEBRIS CHUTE

■ It may be worth your while to set up a debris chute like the one shown in this photo. Locate the window closest to the demolition work, remove the screen or storm window, and temporarily attach a tarp to the inside wall or window casement with duct tape. Fan out the tarp on the exterior and simply throw or shovel debris out the window. A wheelbarrow directly under the window will make it easy to cart the debris away. Cover nearby shrubs with plywood to prevent damage.

Installing Base Cabinets

TOOLS

- Stud finder
- Level
- Driver/drill and bits
- Circular saw or table saw
- Screwdriver
- Clamps

Replacing cabinets is the biggest step in an accessible-kitchen makeover. No other project will have as big an impact on access and ease of use as a new cabinet configuration. And, no other project is as costly: Easily half the cost of the average kitchen remodel job is for the cabinets. Naturally, you want to protect this investment, and that means having the cabinets installed by a professional. Besides the cost issue, installing cabinets is a fine art: The cabinets must be shoehorned into an exact space with little or no clearance. In essence, the job is a large, complicated built-in.

This is not to say that cabinets can't be installed by a homeowner...it's just that the skills and the tools required are many. First, you need to be knowledgeable about cabinet construction so that you can take one apart and modify it if necessary (something an installer often needs to do). Second, you need finely tuned woodworking skills, including scribing, cutting, planing and fitting parts together, mitering and coping molding—even expertise in finishing is also needed. Add to that the required basic and advanced framing skills, and it's easy to see why using a pro makes sense.

Cabinets are usually shipped directly to your door from the manufacturer. When the shipment arrives, check each package carefully for signs of damage before accepting shipment. If you find damage, open the package with the delivery person present. Note any broken items on the bill of lading and contact the distributor or manufacturer for a replacement. Do not uncrate the rest of the cabinets at this time, as the packaging often has the part numbers you'll need to identify which cabinet goes where.

Remove doors and drawers. Cabinets are installed by securing them to the wall studs and to each other through their face frames. In order to fasten and clamp these together, the first step is to remove all of the doors and drawers, as shown in the middle photo.

Level cabinet. A successful cabinet installation begins by identifying the highest point on the floor. This is the starting point for all layout and measurement. Use a bubble level or laser level to find this

and mark the high point on the walls. All your base cabinets will be installed at this higher point. In most cases, the first base cabinet installed will be a corner cabinet (if applicable). If there isn't a corner cabinet (as is the case here), start at one wall and work toward the other end. Make sure to install a filler strip if necessary; see the sidebar below. Since the first cabinet will serve as the foundation for the rest of the installation, spend plenty of time shimming the cabinet until it's both level and plumb.

Shim and secure the cabinet. To secure the cabinet, start by locating and marking the wall studs behind the cabinets. Once located, insert shims between the back of the base cabinet and the wall (if any gap exists). Drive screws through the back of the cabinet (and shims, if applicable), and into wall studs, as shown in the middle left photo.

Continue adding cabinets. With the first cabinet level and

plumb, cabinets can be added. Shim each cabinet as necessary to level the top of the cabinet from side to side and from front to back, and check to make sure the cabinet front is plumb. Clamp the face frames of the cabinets together (as shown in the top right photo), drill pilot holes through the edges of the face frames, and drive long screws through one face frame and into the other. Add all of the standard base cabinets in turn. If any end panels are specified (inset photo above right), attach them as needed.

FILLER STRIPS AND RAISED TOEKICKS

Filler strips: Since cabinets come in standard sizes and kitchens do not, there will inevitably be gaps between cabinets and walls—sometimes even between cabinets, because of the configuration. Here's where filler strips come in. Filler strips are just planks of wood finished to match your cabinets. The strip attaches with screws to the closest cabinet to the wall. When done correctly, the cabinets will look like they were custom-built on site to fit from wall to wall.

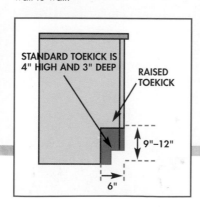

STANDARD TOEKICK IS 4" HIGH AND 3" DEEP

RAISED TOEKICK

9"–12"

6"

FILLER STRIP

WALL

FILLER STRIPS ATTACH TO CABINET FACE FRAME

Raised toekick: A standard toekick (the recess at the bottom of a cabinet) is 4" high and 3" deep. It creates toe room if you stand close to a cabinet. Unfortunately, this "standard" doesn't work for someone in a wheelchair. If you want wheelchair access, ask the cabinetmaker to raise the toekick, as illustrated in the left drawing. Note that all cabinet manufacturers do offer this modification.

Raising a Dishwasher

Tired of bending over to place or remove dishes from your dishwasher? So are a lot of other people. That's why raising a dishwasher has become increasingly popular in kitchens everywhere—and for cooks of all ages and abilities. The amount you need to raise a dishwasher to make a profound difference isn't much—typically 9" to 12". But this 9" to 12" is too much for the average countertop that all dishwashers are designed to fit under. It's important to realize that your countertop, as well as the cabinetry, will have to be modified. This is not a big deal for a new cabinet installation, but is downright nasty for an existing kitchen. If you want to raise an existing dishwasher, consult a kitchen design professional to see what your options are.

the adjacent cabinetry with L-brackets (top right photo).

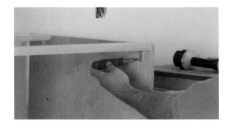

Add countertop cleats. Since you can't set a countertop directly on your dishwasher, you'll have to add a pair of cleats to the front and back top edge of the dishwasher opening, as shown in the photo above.

Hook up plumbing and electrical. Before you can install the dishwasher, you'll need to cut access holes in the cabinet for the waste and supply lines and possibly for the power cable. Slip these lines through the holes and slide the dishwasher in the opening. Level the dishwasher and hook up plumbing and electrical (bottom right photos).

Build and install platform. The first step in raising a dishwasher is to build and install a platform to support the appliance. See page 58 for typical platform construction. Once built, slide the platform in place (bottom left photo), and secure it to

Modifying a Base Cabinet

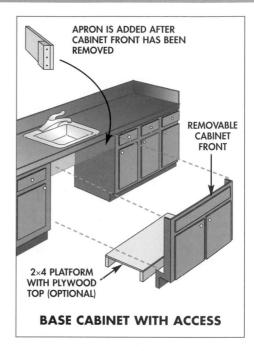

APRON IS ADDED AFTER CABINET FRONT HAS BEEN REMOVED

REMOVABLE CABINET FRONT

2×4 PLATFORM WITH PLYWOOD TOP (OPTIONAL)

BASE CABINET WITH ACCESS

Depending on your (or your cabinet installer's) woodworking skills, almost any sink or cooktop base can be modified for wheelchair access. On a new cabinet install this is easy, since most cabinet manufacturers offer either a removable cabinet front (as shown here) or a pre-made accessible cabinet (like the one shown on page 39). To modify an existing cabinet, you'll first need to remove the base cabinet. Do this by removing the screws that secure the sink base face frame to the adjoining cabinets. What to do next depends on cabinet construction. In most cases, you'll need to remove the sink and faucet along with the wall screws that attach the base to studs. Then free the face frame from the cabinet itself and remove it. To remove the rest of the cabinet, you'll likely destroy the cabinet in the process. But you won't need it anyway. Also, if the flooring doesn't run under the sink base, install flooring to match the existing kitchen floor.

Install the apron. Now that the hard work is done, building the modified front is easy. Just make an apron (as illustrated in the drawing above right) to fit between the cabinets. Cut it wide enough to conceal the sink, and add cleats to the ends to make it easy to attach to the adjoining cabinets, as shown in the bottom left photo.

Add the panel. Now measure the opening and cut a panel to conceal the plumbing lines (if desired), as shown in the bottom right photo. The panel rests against the inside face of the apron and can either rest on the floor or be attached to a cleat screwed to the floor.

Installing Wall Cabinets

TOOLS

- Stud finder
- Level
- Driver/drill and bits
- Circular saw
- Miter saw
- Screwdriver
- Clamps
- Air nailer (optional)

Once all the base cabinets are in and the countertop (if applicable) has been installed, the next step is to tackle the wall cabinets. Although in some installations it can be best to install the wall cabinets first, this isn't possible with the cabinets shown here, since some of the cabinets rest directly on top of the countertop. Specialty cabinets (such as a tall wall oven cabinet or pantry) are usually installed before the wall cabinets are installed. These heavy units are jockeyed carefully into position, made level and plumb, and secured to the adjoining cabinets.

Attach cabinets to studs. To get consistent spacing between the countertop and the wall cabinets, consider using spacer blocks cut from scrap wood, as shown in the bottom left photo. These spacers help support the cabinet so it can be leveled and secured to the wall, as you did with base cabinets.

Secure cabinets to each other. Once the first wall cabinet is secured to the wall, it can be attached to the adjoining cabinet, like the wall oven unit shown in the bottom right photo. Careful measuring and lay-out is called for here, as it's easy to drill through a cabinet side and miss the adjoining cabinet's frame entirely.

Continue adding cabinets. Adjoining cabinets are installed in a similar manner, always using the spacer blocks whenever possible for uniform spacing (top photo). Instead of installing cabinets one at a time, some installers level and plumb sections of cabinets in groups and fasten them together. Then they temporarily attach a cleat to the wall directly below the line where the wall cabinets will be installed. With the help of an assistant or two, the assembled unit is lifted up onto the cleat. Then the cabinet is checked for level one more time and secured to the wall studs. When strong backs are available, this method can speed up installation.

The most secure way to attach molding to a cabinet top is to cut and attach blocking. This blocking is just scraps of 2×4 that are cut to fit behind the top lip of the cabinet. The blocking is secured to the back of the top cabinet lip with glue and nails, as shown in the bottom photo.

Install blocking. Once all of the wall cabinets are mounted, you can install moldings, if applicable. The molding shown here is actually made up of three pieces plus blocking, as illustrated in the drawing at right. The molding consists of an extension, the crown molding, and a detail piece.

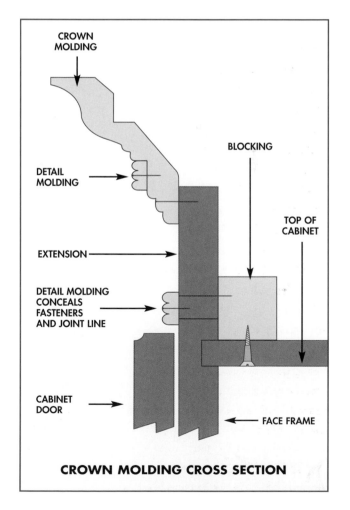

CROWN MOLDING

DETAIL MOLDING

EXTENSION

DETAIL MOLDING CONCEALS FASTENERS AND JOINT LINE

CABINET DOOR

BLOCKING

TOP OF CABINET

FACE FRAME

CROWN MOLDING CROSS SECTION

Add extension molding.
With the blocking in place, you can cut and attach your extension molding (if applicable). Since most modern kitchen cabinet designs call for cabinets that extend all the way to the ceiling, extension moldings are necessary for most installs. The extension molding rests on top of the cabinet face frame and is mitered at the corners as needed. Secure the molding to the blocking with glue and nails. The best tool for attaching any molding is an air-powered nailer like the one shown in the top left photo (you can find these at most rental centers). An air nailer will drive and set the nail exactly where you want it with the pull of a trigger. Sure, you can attach molding with a hammer and nails, but the chances of dinging the molding are extremely high. Also, since a finish nailer can be used one-handed, your other hand is free to hold the molding in place—not so with a hammer and nails.

Attach the crown. After you've attached an extension (if applicable), you can cut your crown molding. Cutting crown is tricky. It's a good idea to practice your first cuts on scrap until you get the hang of it. In general, you want to place the molding upside down and backwards on your miter saw when cutting. Start by attaching the crown to the extension as shown in the top right photo. Then nail the top edge into any ceiling joists, if possible. If you need to join together two lengths of molding, cut the ends at opposing 45-degree miters to create an almost invisible "scarf" joint. When possible, cut miters first and then trim the molding to length, always erring on the long side.

Attach the detail strip. Much of the crown molding available from cabinet manufacturers comes in two pieces: the crown molding and a detail strip that is attached to a flat on the molding. The system allows the manufacturers to offer different looks using the same crown molding. Cut the detail strips to length, mitering the end or ends as needed. Then secure them to the flat section of the crown molding with glue and brads, as shown in the bottom photo.

When all the trim is in place, re-install the doors and then add the cabinet hardware (page 105), along with any specialty items such as pull-out bins (page 104) or pull-down shelving (pages 102–103).

Extenders and Step Stools

Successful aging in place can hinge on lots of little things, as well as big issues like makeovers. After all, it's tough to maintain independence if you can't reach down to put on your socks...press hard to open a jar...get a grip on turning a house key in a lock. Fortunately, though, there are dozens of aids available to help with such tasks.

Two of the most useful everyday accessories are reach-extenders and safety footstools. Everyone sometimes has trouble reaching and holding things that are up high and/or heavy. That's where extenders (like the ones in the photos on this page) can be handy helpers. Some are 20" inches long, some will fold out to 30" or

more; some have grasping "jaws" that you operate with a hand-trigger, some use suction cups or magnets to reach and hold items. The versions pictured are marketed by North Coast Medical, Inc. (www.beabletodo.com). Their website and print catalog are full of aids for everyday tasks.

SAFER STEP STOOLS

Reaching and grasping things sometimes means moving your whole body closer to an object—but conventional step stools can be precarious. For extra security and support, a footstool from Duro-Med Industries can be the answer. Its tall handrail (see photo) attaches to a non-skid, non-slip stepstool, elevating you 9" to reach those upper shelves, while still giving you the safety of a handle to hold. The footstool with handle is available from a number of retail sources, including direct marketer Walter Drake (www.wdrake.com).

Pull-Down Shelving

TOOLS

- Tape measure
- Awl
- Drill and bits
- Screwdriver
- Adjustable wrench

If there's one cabinet accessory that just about anyone can appreciate, it's the pull-down shelving shown here, manufactured by the ingenious folks at Rev-A-Shelf (www.rev-a-shelf.com). The shelves pictured are designed to fit into a 24" wall cabinet (we installed ours in a laundry room). Rev-A-Shelf's pull-down shelving unit lowers hard-to-reach items a full 10", while extending out 14 3/4" from the cabinet. The unit's unique gas-assisted lifting/lowering mechanism provides excellent stability through the entire range of motion.

Assemble the shelving. The first step to installing a pull-down shelving unit is to assemble the unit according to the manufacturer's directions, as shown in the bottom left photo. This is just a matter of attaching the sides to the rods that connect them together.

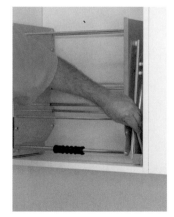

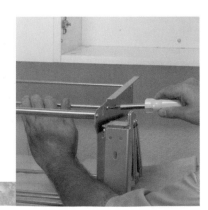

Drill mounting holes. Once it's assembled, you can locate and drill the holes for the mounting brackets that secure the unit to the cabinet. Use the dimensions provided in the instructions or simply insert the unit (with brackets attached) in the cabinet; then mark through the mounting holes onto the cabinet bottom with an awl, as we did in the middle photo. Once located, remove the unit and drill the holes with the bit specified by the manufacturer (inset).

Attach the brackets. Attach the mounting brackets to the inside of the cabinet as shown in the top left photo. Use the fasteners provided with the shelf, and tighten them securely with a screwdriver and an adjustable wrench.

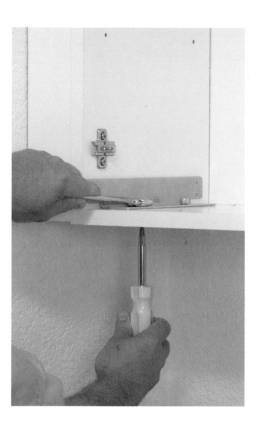

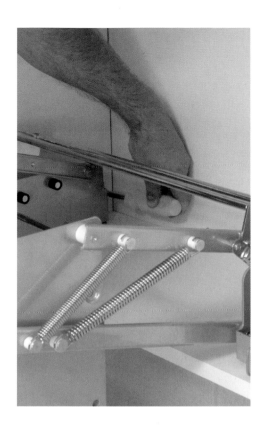

Attach the shelving to the brackets. With both brackets in place, lift the unit up and into the cabinet and position it on the mounting bracket so the mounting holes in the unit and bracket align. Insert the fasteners provided into the front of the bracket (as shown in the bottom left photo) and then into the rear of the bracket (as shown in the top left photo). Don't tighten them fully at this time. Repeat this for the remaining bracket. With all fasteners in place, go back and fully tighten them.

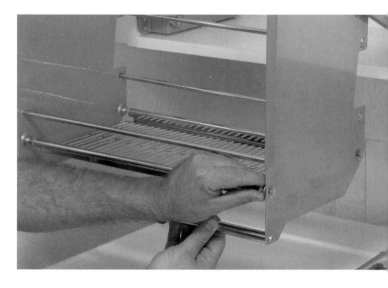

Install the wire shelves. All that's left is to add the wire shelves. The shelves shown here have spring-loaded plungers in the ends that fit into holes in the sides of the unit. After you've inserted the plunger units in the ends of the wire shelves, install the shelves in the unit, as shown in the bottom right photo. Test the operation by gripping the handle and pulling the shelving gently forward.

Pull-Out Bins

TOOLS

- Tape measure
- Awl
- Drill and bits
- Screwdriver

Bins that pull out of a cabinet not only are back savers, but they also maximize the space by making everything within them accessible. Depending on the configuration, these can be used to store dry goods, pots and pans—even recycling and waste. These handy units are from Rev-A-Shelf (www.rev-a-shelf.com).

hole locations with an awl. If there is no template, position the slide in the cabinet per the directions so it's centered from side to side. Then use an awl or pencil to mark the locations of the mounting holes, as shown in the bottom left photo. Once marked, remove the template or slide and drill the recommended size hole. Then reposition the slide and secure it to the bottom with the screws provided (top right photo).

Locate and attach the slide. Follow the manufacturer's instructions to locate and install the pull-out slide. This may be a single unit (as shown), or a pair of glides that attach to the inside faces of the cabinet. In some cases the manufacturer provides a paper template that you place in the cabinet; then you poke through the mounting

Add supports and containers. Now you can install the support brackets and containers. The support brackets typically snap into plastic retainers on the base of the slide, as shown in the photo above. Then just slip the containers into the support brackets (bottom right photo).

New Hardware

Although it may seem like a small detail, the hardware you choose for new or existing cabinets can have a big effect on both the overall appearance of the cabinets and their accessibility. Cabinet hardware for the mature home should be pulls instead of hard-to-grasp knobs. For each pull to function properly—and look good—it must be carefully positioned and precisely installed. (The only advantage a knob has over a pull is that it's easier to install.) Pulls can cause headaches: The distance between each end isn't standard; the distance might be 3", 3^1/$_4$", 3^1/$_2$", and so on. Also, if you're purchasing pulls for drawers with false fronts, you'll need to pick up some longer screws. Most home centers have specialty drawer

TOOLS

• Electric drill
• Screwdriver
• Shop-made guide

screws that feature snap-off threads that can be customized to fit your drawers.

Drill holes and install the pulls.
When it's time to drill mounting holes for your new hardware, use a drilling guide (see below), as position is critical. Hold the drilling guide in place on the corner of a door or drawer so its cleats butt up against the edges of the part. Then drill through the holes in the guide and into the door frame or drawer. Make sure the door is open (bottom left photo) to prevent the bit from drilling into the cabinet face frame. Remove the drilling jig and attach the pull (middle photo).

DRILLING GUIDE

■ Accurate placement of cabinet hardware is something you notice only when a knob, hinge, or pull is out of alignment. Then, it sticks out like the proverbial sore thumb. To prevent this, it's worth the time and effort to make a simple drilling guide. The guide is just a piece of ^{1}/$_4$" plywood or hardboard with cleats on both faces to serve as lips to automatically position the guide for drilling. Once you've decided on placement for the hardware, measure the distance up from the bottom and offset from the adjacent edge; transfer these measurements to the guide (see the drawing at right). Then drill the desired-size mounting hole in the guide at this location.

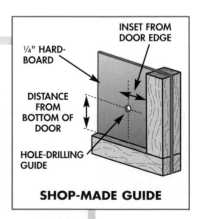

INSET FROM DOOR EDGE

^{1}/$_4$" HARD-BOARD

DISTANCE FROM BOTTOM OF DOOR

HOLE-DRILLING GUIDE

SHOP-MADE GUIDE

A Solid-Surface Countertop

When you're ready to upgrade your countertop for looks and performance, consider solid surface. Solid-surface countertops can be a blend of natural materials and pure acrylic polymers, or be 100% acrylic, like the stunning Staron by Samsung used here (www.getstaron.com). Besides coming in a huge array of colors and patterns, what makes a solid-surface countertop unique is exactly what the name says: It's solid all the way through. This is different from laminate or tile countertops, where cutting produces a raw, exposed edge of plywood or particleboard. When you cut into solid-surface material, you get solid surface. And this means you can cut it, rout it, carve it, add decorative inlays—even sandblast it. If you want to inlay a complex pattern on the edge or rout drainage grooves into the surface near the sink, there's no problem. In addition to the flexibility of design and construction that solid-surface materials offer, they are non-porous, resist stains well, and are easy to clean. And because of its solid composition, the surface can be periodically renewed if necessary.

Sheets of solid-surface material are precut into standard lengths at the factories and then shipped to trained professionals who fabricate and install the product. Be aware that a solid-surface material can be purchased only through a distributor, and must be shaped

and installed by a certified fabricator/installer. That's because cutting, routing, and joining solid-surface materials takes skill and experience—it's best left to a professional.

Trim countertop as needed. Even with the most careful templating (see the opposite page), odds are that one or more of the back or side edges will need to be fine-tuned for a perfect fit. In most cases, the installer will handle this on the spot by removing the offending material with a belt sander or laminate trimmer, as shown in the middle photo. For large variations, they may have to return the top to the factory, but they'll do everything to prevent this once the countertop is on site.

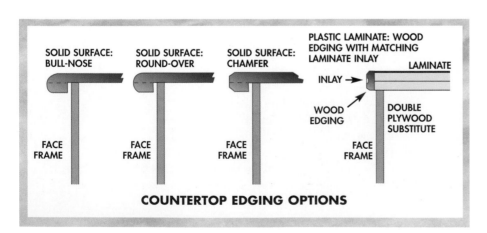

SOLID SURFACE: BULL-NOSE

SOLID SURFACE: ROUND-OVER

SOLID SURFACE: CHAMFER

PLASTIC LAMINATE: WOOD EDGING WITH MATCHING LAMINATE INLAY

LAMINATE

INLAY →

WOOD EDGING

DOUBLE PLYWOOD SUBSTITUTE

FACE FRAME

FACE FRAME

FACE FRAME

FACE FRAME

COUNTERTOP EDGING OPTIONS

TEMPLATING A COUNTERTOP

■ The first step to fabricating a solid-surface countertop is called templating. Once your cabinets are installed, your local authorized dealer will send out a certified installer to make a template of your new countertop. This is usually done with thin strips of wood glued together to define the perimeter of the countertop Once the template is made, it goes back to the factory, where it serves as a template to shape the actual countertop.

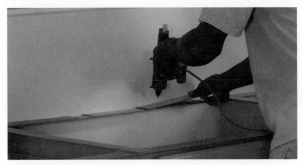

Attach strips to cabinets. The installer starts by temporarily attaching thin wood strips to your cabinet tops with hot-melt glue.

Continue around perimeter. The installer then continues working around the perimeter of the cabinets, cutting and gluing strips together as needed.

Add strips where cabinets join. As the installer continues working, strips are cut and glued together wherever cabinets join together.

Measure for overhang. The installer then measures and marks the template for the desired amount of overhang, and trims strips as needed.

Label transitions. Wherever the countertop changes directions (like the point where the peninsula begins), marks are made on the template to identify this transition.

Mark centerlines as needed. Finally, the installer will lay out the location of the sink and any other necessary cutouts (such as an island cooktop). Armed with this template and the pattern for any openings, he returns to the factory, where the top is fabricated to perfectly match the template.

Position the countertop. An installation crew will show up along with the countertop on the installation date. The final placement of the countertop is sort of a wrestling match between the installers and the countertop. This is especially true with an L- or U-shaped countertop that must be wedged in between cabinets. The weight and awkwardness of the countertop adds to the drama. What makes it so difficult is that the edges of the countertop can easily damage the walls and cabinets. Here's where the experience of the installers will be truly evident.

Install any additional sections. If there are multiple countertop sections to install, these go in next. Some are simple to install, like the countertop that covers the dishwasher, as shown in the middle right photo. Still, simple pieces like this may require trimming to fit perfectly.

Secure the top to the cabinets. When the installers are pleased with the fit, they'll secure the countertop to the cabinets. The countertop material used will determine how this is done. On some material, the fabricator will glue strips of wood underneath the countertop where the cabinets join together to provide a fastening surface for screws. To secure the countertop, an installer drives screws up through the corner brackets (attached to the cabinet for this purpose) and into the wood strips, as shown in the bottom photo. Alternatively, if fastening strips weren't used, the front edge of the countertop is propped up temporarily and a few dollops of silicone caulk are applied to the front top edge of the cabinets. Since a solid-surface top is heavy, this is all it takes to secure it: The weight of the top itself helps hold it in place.

Check for gaps and shim if needed. After all the countertop sections have been installed and secured, a quality-minded installation crew will carefully inspect the job for any possible problems. If they find any gaps between the bottom of the countertop and the top of the base cabinets, they'll insert shims to fill the gap, as shown in the top photo. This will prevent the countertop from flexing and possibly cracking over time.

Seal at the backsplash. The final step is to seal the back edge of the countertop with silicone caulk (bottom photo). The installer should do this whether or not a backsplash is to be installed. Sealing between the countertop and the wall is insurance against moisture damage. If desired, you can have them fabricate and install a solid-surface backsplash, as illustrated in the drawing at right.

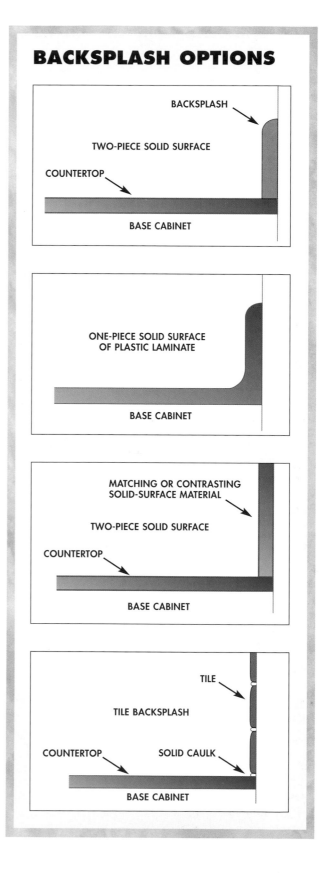

BACKSPLASH OPTIONS

BACKSPLASH

TWO-PIECE SOLID SURFACE

COUNTERTOP

BASE CABINET

ONE-PIECE SOLID SURFACE OF PLASTIC LAMINATE

BASE CABINET

MATCHING OR CONTRASTING SOLID-SURFACE MATERIAL

TWO-PIECE SOLID SURFACE

COUNTERTOP

BASE CABINET

TILE

TILE BACKSPLASH

COUNTERTOP

SOLID CAULK

BASE CABINET

Open Shelving

Open shelving is a perfect fit in any accessible room. That's because there are no doors or drawers to impede access to the contents. The open shelving unit shown here is straightforward in design and can be adapted to fit almost any space. You can design one to shoehorn into a small space, like the one between the low-threshold shower unit and nearby wall (as shown in the top photo), or build one to fit almost anywhere. The shelving unit shown here consists of two sides, a top and bottom, a back, and a set of shelves that rest on cleats, as illustrated in the drawing at right. To conceal the cleats, a face frame (trim) is attached to the front of the shelving unit.

TOOLS

- Tape measure
- Straightedge or framing square
- Air nailer (optional)
- Hammer and nail set
- Circular saw or table saw
- Screwdriver

Lay out the shelves. To build an open shelving unit, first measure your opening (if applicable) and decide on dimensions and the number of shelves and their

spacing. Cut the sides, top, and bottom to size. Next, butt the sides together with the long edges touching, and measure and mark the desired spacing for the shelf cleats. Use a straightedge or framing square and a pencil to mark lines across both sides, as shown in the top right photo.

Install the shelf cleats. Cut the cleats to size and attach them to the sides. Align the top edge of a cleat with a line you marked on a side, and fasten the cleat to the side. You can use an air nailer for this (as shown in the bottom photo), a hammer and nails, or screws and a screwdriver. Repeat for all of the shelf cleats.

Assemble the unit. Now you can assemble the unit. Start by attaching the sides to the top and bottom. Here again, you can do this with nails or screws. With the unit assembled, check the fit of the shelves, as shown in the top left photo. If the fit is good, secure these to the unit by driving nails up through the cleats and into the bottom of each shelf.

Install the face frame or trim. To complete the shelving unit, cut and trim molding or other stock to cover the exposed ends of the shelf cleats. Attach the face frame or trim to the unit with nails or brads (top right photo). Set nail heads below the surface with a hammer and nail set, and fill the holes with putty. When dry, sand smooth and apply the finish of your choice. Install the shelving by screwing through the sides or back into the wall or wall studs, as shown in the bottom right photo.

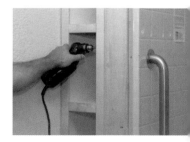

Add the back. With the shelves in place, measure the unit and cut a back to fit from 1/4" plywood. This can be a single piece, or multiple pieces as shown in the bottom left photo. Fasten the back or back pieces to the back of the shelving unit with nails or brads.

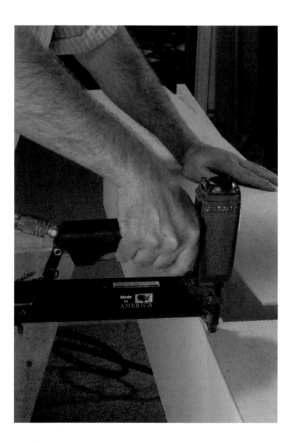

WALLS, STEPS & HALLWAYS

6

Steps and hallways are intended to help us get into places, but they can have the opposite effect. If you use a cane, a walker, or a wheelchair—or if you simply have a stiff knee—many homes are tough to enter, or simply off-limits. Your access might be barred entirely by steps; if you are able to enter, the standard narrow hallways can prevent you from accessing many of the rooms, or from turning around in a wheelchair.

In this chapter, we'll show what's involved with moving walls to widen a hallway so that you can tackle the job yourself or hire a licensed contractor to do it for you. We'll cover basic drywall technique, and then show how to install handrails. We'll also go step-by-step with installing a maintenance-free wall covering called tileboard, which helps protect against dents and dings. Finally, we'll look at replacing steps with a ramp or berm.

Widening a Hallway

TOOLS

- Pry bar and putty knife
- Utility knife
- Handsaw, reciprocating saw, or circular saw
- Cat's paw
- Hammer
- Cold chisel
- Screwdriver
- Hydraulic jacks (for wall brace)

To widen a hallway for greater access, the first step is to remove one of the existing walls. Whenever possible, choose the "simplest" wall to move—that's the wall with the fewest openings and electrical lines. Since we wanted to create a turning radius for wheelchairs by angling the doorways into the guest bath and master bedroom—and widen those doorways at the same time—we didn't have a practical choice about which wall to move for our hallway makeover (pages 68–69). Knocking down and moving walls is a project for veteran do-it-yourselfers only. If any of this makes you nervous, hire a licensed contractor.

For many homeowners, it's hard to resist the temptation to pick up a sledgehammer and start knocking out a wall. But it's important to first prepare the area for demolition. A well-placed fan and drop cloths will help minimize the dust problem, and a debris chute (see page 93) will make short work of clearing out and cleaning up the mess.

Remove the doors and trim. To remove a wall, begin by using a pry bar and wide-blade putty knife to remove all the trim (door trim, baseboard, and ceiling molding if applicable), as shown in the top photo. (Make sure to

wear gloves and eye protection when doing any demolition work.) Next, knock out the door-hinge pins (bottom left photo) with a hammer and cold chisel and remove any doors.

Remove the door jambs. Before you remove the door jambs, you might want to remove the hinge-mounting screws first. In many doors, one or more of these screws is longer, to pass through the jamb and into the wall stud. It's easier to unscrew these long screws than it is to pry them out. Use a pry bar to lever the bottom of the jamb out and then pull it out as shown in the middle photo. If you won't be reusing the jambs, it's often easiest to cut them in half at their midpoint first and pry out the separate pieces.

Cut the drywall joints. To remove drywall, first cut it into manageable sections so you can tear it off and dispose of it. It's easy to get carried away with this, to just grab a section of drywall and rip it off the studs. But before you do this, slice through the taped joints at the corners of intersecting walls and at the ceiling with a utility knife, as shown in the photo at right. If you don't sever these joints, odds are you'll rip the paper facing off the adjoining drywall surfaces and create additional work for yourself.

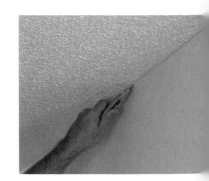

Remove the drywall.
Once the drywall has been cut and the adjoining tape joints cut, you can remove the drywall. The first area to work on requires the most patience and finesse—this is any section that butts up against or is next to an area of wall that you don't want to remove. Insert a pry bar under the drywall and carefully pry back the drywall until you can slip your hand under it. Then carefully pull the drywall away from the studs, as shown in the top left photo. For drywall that is next to areas that are coming down, you can be more aggressive. As long as you're sure that there are no hidden surprises in the wall, you can use the claws of a hammer to puncture the drywall. The claws also provide an excellent purchase to pull the wall covering off. Regardless of how you remove drywall, be sure to wear a quality dust mask to protect your lungs from construction dust.

Disconnect any wiring. If there are receptacles or switches in the wall or wall section to be removed, identify which circuit breaker or fuse controls their power and shut off and tag the breaker or fuse. Verify that the power is off by flipping any switches to make sure the device they control is without power, and check the receptacles with a circuit tester or multimeter. Mark

each cable and then draw a wiring diagram of the switch or receptacle connections. If necessary, label the actual wires to make reconnection easier. Then disconnect any switches or receptacles (photo above), and push the cables up through the top plate and into the ceiling (photo at right). You'll pull these back down through the new top plate once it's installed; see the sidebar on page 118.

BRACING CEILINGS WHEN REMOVING WALLS

■ Whenever a remodeling job requires you to remove a load-bearing wall or remove more than one stud in a load-bearing wall, you'll need to brace the ceiling. Temporary supports or braces bear the weight the wall normally would until a new wall is installed. How you install a brace will depend on whether the ceiling joists run perpendicular or parallel to the wall you're working on, as illustrated in the drawing at right.

The easiest way to support the wall is to build a T-shaped brace, as shown in the photo at left. The brace is just three 4×4's, joined at the top with framing connectors, and is pressed into place with hydraulic jacks. When installing the brace, take care not to apply too much pressure with the jacks or you'll damage the ceiling. You're just trying to support the ceiling here, not raise it.

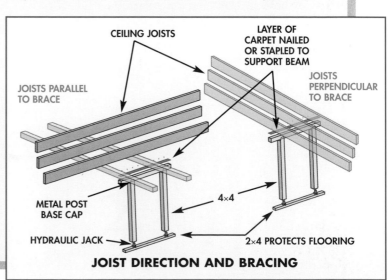

JOIST DIRECTION AND BRACING

Cut through studs.

For load-bearing walls, make sure that you build and install braces on both sides of the wall you're working on before cutting any studs (see the sidebar on page 115). A short "tool-box" saw (top left photo) will quickly zip through the studs and fits easily between them. If you're planning on reusing any of the studs, make your cut near either the top or bottom plate. If not, cut the studs in the middle; this gives you the best "handle" to remove each piece.

Remove the studs. After you've cut the wall studs, they can be removed. Wearing leather gloves, grip each piece, bend it back toward you, and twist it, as shown in the bottom photo. In most cases, this will release the stud from the nails holding it in place. If not, lever it back and forth while twisting at the same time.

Stubborn studs may need a pry bar or crowbar to convince them to give up their grip. Be careful of exposed nails in the top and sole plates. Bend over any exposed nails to reduce the chances of injury.

Cut and remove top and bottom plates.

Cutting through a top plate is an awkward job with either a hand- or power saw. A short "toolbox" saw with its aggressive teeth is a good choice to make the cut. Hold the saw upside down as shown in the top right photo, and take firm strokes. To keep from scoring the ceiling, wrap a layer or two of duct

tape around the tip of the saw; this way if it does make contact with the ceiling, the tip won't cause damage. A crowbar or pry bar is usually required to break the top plate free of the ceiling joists. To prevent damage to the ceiling, insert a stiff putty knife between the pry bar and the ceiling and make sure to pick a leverage spot directly under a ceiling joist. The final step to removing a wall or section of a wall is to cut (middle photo) and remove the bottom plate. Just like the top plate, the bottom plate will be firmly fixed in place. Use a pry bar or crowbar to lever it out.

Framing a New Hallway

TOOLS

- Tape measure
- Hammer
- Circular saw or handsaw
- Utility knife
- Chalk line and plumb bob
- Straightedge of framing square
- Air nailer (optional)
- Drill and bits

Building a partition wall is fairly straightforward. The framing is simple because partition walls are non-load-bearing and aren't designed to support any substantial weight. That's not to say you don't have to be careful—any wall you put up should be well made, firmly attached, plumb, and straight.

Lay out the top plate. The first step in building a partition wall is to lay out the top plate on the ceiling. To do this, first measure and mark the start and stop points of the top plate. Then stretch a chalk line between these points and snap a line, as shown in the bottom left photo, to define its location. Repeat this for the other edge of the top plate so it's clear where it will be installed.

Cut ceiling drywall as needed. Since code requires that wall framing

attach to ceiling framing (the ceiling joists), cut and remove ceiling drywall as needed to expose the ceiling joists, as shown in the top right photo. Once the drywall is removed, go back and re-snap your reference chalk lines.

Install the top plate. The next step is to make and install the top plate. The length of this will depend on the wall that you're adding. Once you've cut it to length, attach it to the ceiling joists as shown in the bottom right photo. The best way to do this is to attach one end and then align the edges of the top plate with your chalk lines you made earlier on the ceiling joists. Once aligned, fasten the other end and secure the plate to any joists between the ends of the top plate.

Transfer the top plate location to floor.
Once you've installed the top plate, you can transfer its location to the floor with a plumb bob so that you can locate the bottom plate. Hold the string of the plumb bob up against the top plate at one corner—the plumb bob will hover directly over the corresponding point on the floor, as shown in the top left photo. Mark this location and move the plumb bob to the adjacent corner. Repeat on the opposite end.

Lay out the bottom plate. If you took your time with the plumb bob as described here, you'll end up with a series of dots on the floor. Use a straightedge or framing square, (top right photo) to connect the dots and lay out the bottom plate on the floor.

DEALING WITH WIRING

If the wall you're moving or adding needs wiring run through it, you'll need to take care of this before you attach a wall covering. If you're moving a wall and have disconnected and tucked the wiring up in the ceiling as described on page 115, all you need to do is drill new access holes, route the cable or cables through the holes, and reconnect them. Although this sounds simple, it usually isn't, for two reasons. First, unless you have access to the wiring from below, you (or a helper) will need to go up into the ceiling (or down under the floor) to snake the cables through the new access holes. Second, depending on how far you moved the wall and the amount of slack in the cables, the cables may not be long enough for you to install the new electrical boxes at the correct height specified by the electrical code. If the cables are too short, you (or a licensed electrician) will need to install junction boxes in the attic or basement for splicing in a longer cable.

Drill access holes for cable. Locate and drill cable access holes as needed in the new top plate. To keep from weakening the top plate, make sure to drill holes centered on the width of the 2×4; drill holes only large enough for the cable to pass through.

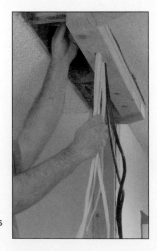

Pull cable down through access holes. With the holes drilled, you can snake the cables through the holes and down into the wall. If you don't have access to the cables, have a helper locate the cables and push them through the top plate.

Install the bottom plates. Once the bottom plates have been laid out, you can cut and attach them to the floor. How you attach them will depend on the subfloor. On wood subfloors, you can secure the bottom plates with nails or screws. Whenever possible, nail or screw through the subfloor and into the floor joists. For concrete subfloors, you can attach the bottom plates with a power-actuated nailer that "shoots" nails into the concrete, or use concrete screws (like Tap-cons), as shown in the top photo.

Locate and install the wall studs. With the top and bottom plates in place, you can add the wall studs between them. Measure and cut one stud at a time, since odds are that the ceiling and floor aren't precisely parallel to each other. Cut the studs to fit snugly between the plates—a tight fit helps hold the stud in place for nailing. Toenail each of the studs to the top plate and bottom plate, as shown in the middle photo. If you have access to an air nailer, you'll really appreciate how easily it handles this often-frustrating task (you can rent air nailers and compressors at most rental centers).

Install transition studs.
The final framing step is to add any studs for intersecting walls, corners (as shown in the bottom photo), or rough openings for windows or doors (see pages 130–132 on how to frame a door opening). Here again, it's best to measure, cut, and install one piece at a time to compensate for uneven walls, floors, and ceilings. When framing is complete, have your local building inspector check your work before applying a wall covering (see pages 120–121 on how to install drywall).

Drywall

TOOLS

- Drill and driver bit
- Straightedge or drywall T-square
- Putty knife and utility knife
- Tin snips
- Drywall knives
- Sponge or sanding frame

Many makeover projects require removing and installing wall coverings. The easiest wall covering to install is drywall. We recommend 1/2" drywall whenever possible, as it holds up better over time. When installing drywall in rooms where moisture is present, make sure to use moisture-resistant drywall. It's easy to identify from standard drywall by its green color (see page 124 for an example of this).

Install the drywall.

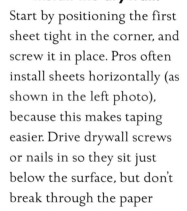

Start by positioning the first sheet tight in the corner, and screw it in place. Pros often install sheets horizontally (as shown in the left photo), because this makes taping easier. Drive drywall screws or nails in so they sit just below the surface, but don't break through the paper covering. The second sheet will most likely need to be cut to fit. Carefully measure from the existing sheet to the ceiling or floor on both ends of the panel, and transfer these measurements to a full sheet. Draw a line with a straightedge or make a chalk line, and then cut along this line with a sharp utility knife. Flip the sheet over and lift up one end to snap the sheet. Run your utility knife along the inside crease to cut completely through the sheet. Check the fit of the cut sheet and trim as necessary.

Attach the sheet with drywall screws or nails and continue until the framing is covered.

Tape the joints. To conceal the joints between the sheets of drywall, apply drywall tape over the gaps. Drywall tape may be self-adhesive or non-stick. To apply self-adhesive tape, simply remove the paper backing and press it in place. Non-adhesive tape is applied by first spreading on a thin coat of joint compound and then pressing the tape into the compound with a wide-blade

putty knife, as shown in the top right photo. Exposed corners are best covered with metal corner bead. This is thin, L-shaped metal that's easily cut with tin snips and can be nailed or screwed to the framing members.

Apply the first coat of mud. With all the tape in place, the next step is to apply a first coat of joint compound, commonly called "mud" by the pros. Joint compound comes pre-mixed or in a powder form that you can mix yourself. Apply a generous first coat with a 4"- to 6"-wide drywall knife or putty knife, as shown in the bottom photo. Cover the tape completely, plus all the impressions or "dimples" left by the screws or nails. Inside and outside corners are best done with special drywall tools designed especially for this. Apply the joint compound as smoothly as possible, but don't be too meticulous—you'll remove any high spots before applying the next coat.

Apply the feather coats. Once the first coat of joint compound has dried thoroughly (usually overnight), go over the joints with a stiff-blade putty knife and knock off or scrape away any high spots. Then apply the next coat. Use a wider drywall knife and spread the joint compound over the first coat, as shown in the middle photo. Work the compound gently away from the joint to "feather" it for a smooth transition to the drywall. Multiple thin coats work best here. Let each coat dry, knock off any high spots, and then apply the next. Repeat as necessary to create a flat surface.

Sand or sponge the wall smooth. When the joint compound is completely dry, the final step is to smooth the surface to remove any remaining imperfections. In the past, this was usually done with sandpaper or sanding screen, and created a horrendous mess. A tidier alternative that works great is to smooth the joint compound with a drywall sponge, like the one shown in the top photo. These sponges have a non-abrasive pad glued to one side to quickly flatten high spots. Wet the sponge and wring it out so it's just damp. Then use a swirling motion to smooth the joints. If you've got a lot of drywall to smooth, consider renting a power drywall sander as described in the sidebar below. When the drywall is smooth, roll on a coat of drywall sealer and then apply the decorative wall covering of your choice.

DRYWALL SANDING SYSTEMS

■ If any of your makeover projects involves installing a lot of drywall, consider renting a drywall sanding system like the Porter-Cable unit shown here. The Porter-Cable model 7800 is a variable-speed sander with a built-in dust collection hose that connects to a high-efficiency vacuum. The business end of the sander features easy-to-change sanding pads of varying grits. The vacuum provides 99.85% filtration efficiency that's perfect for capturing fine drywall dust. The vacuum is automatically turned on or off by the sander's power switch. The vacuum stays on an additional 15 seconds after the sander is turned off, to clear the hose. This combination of quick smoothing action coupled with excellent dust collection makes even large smoothing jobs a snap.

Installing Handrails

TOOLS

• Stud finder
• Tape measure
• Drill and bits
• Screwdriver

More than one-third of adults age 65 and over are injured in falls every year, according to the National Center for Injury Control and Prevention. In many cases, these accidents could have been prevented with a handrail. Handrails are also a great aid for anyone with knee or back troubles. Handrails should be installed in every stairway (preferably on both sides) in the home, as well as any location where there are changes in floor levels.

When shopping for handrails, look for those with a rounded design as they tend to fit hands better. Stay away from large handrails that are difficult to grasp; the part you grab should be less than 1 1/2" in diameter. Choose a handrail that can support your weight (most are designed to support around 250 pounds). Handrails are secured to walls via handrail brackets. You can find these at most hardware stores and home centers, along with wood handrails. The brackets should extend the handrail out from the wall at least 1 1/2" to make it easy to grip.

Locate the wall studs. For a handrail to be mounted securely to a wall, the bracket should be secured to the wall studs (whenever possible). You can locate the wall studs with an electronic stud finder, like the one shown in the top right photo. Alternatively, you can attach the brackets to drywall with molly bolts, but this is nowhere near as secure as fastening them to the wall studs.

Locate the mounting bracket. Most handrails are mounted about 34" from the floor. Children or smaller adults may find a secondary handrail useful, as illustrated in the drawing on the opposite page. At a stud location, measure up from the floor and make a mark at 34" to locate the top of the handrail. Then subtract the thickness of your handrail from this and make a mark. This is where you want the top of the mounting bracket. Hold the bracket on the wall so it's centered on a stud location and at the marked height. Then mark the bracket's mounting hole locations on the wall,

as shown in the bottom photo. Repeat for additional brackets; as a general rule, brackets should be installed every other stud (roughly 32" on center).

Install the wall bracket. When you've marked all the bracket mounting holes, drill pilot holes for the screws through the wall covering and into the wall stud. Reposition the handrail bracket and secure it to the wall stud with the screws provided, as shown in the top left photo.

Attach the handrail. All that's left is to attach the handrail to the bracket using the plate and screws provided with the bracket. Since most handrails are made of wood, make sure to first sand them smooth (to avoid splinters), and apply a protective finish before attaching them to the brackets. Choose a flat, satin, or eggshell enamel for this; avoid glossy paint, since it can be slippery. Set the handrail on the bracket. Position a plate under the handrail so it fits over the bracket bottom, and mark the mounting hole locations on the bottom of the handrail. Drill pilot holes and attach the plate to the handrail with the screws provided, as shown in the top right photo.

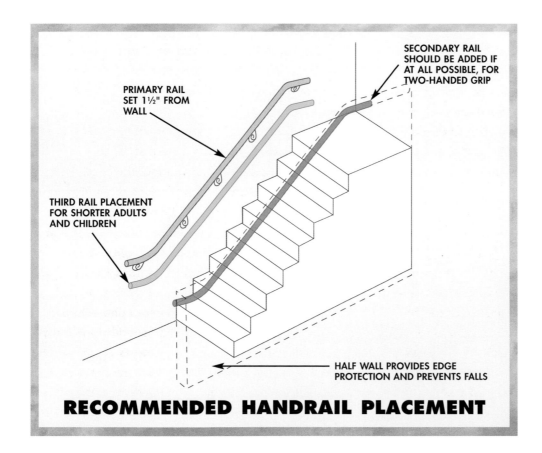

PRIMARY RAIL SET 1½" FROM WALL

SECONDARY RAIL SHOULD BE ADDED IF AT ALL POSSIBLE, FOR TWO-HANDED GRIP

THIRD RAIL PLACEMENT FOR SHORTER ADULTS AND CHILDREN

HALF WALL PROVIDES EDGE PROTECTION AND PREVENTS FALLS

RECOMMENDED HANDRAIL PLACEMENT

Tileboard

Tileboard or decorative paneling is a mature-friendly wall covering for a couple of reasons: It's easy to install, it's virtually maintenance-free, and it can help protect walls against potential damage from walkers and wheelchairs. The tileboard shown here and used in the guest bathroom makeover (page 63) is manufactured by DPI (www.decpanels.com). We used a design from their attractive line called AquaTile, an embossed tile look-alike designed for rooms where moisture is present; the entire DPI line offers many patterns, colors, and textures.

Before installation, all decorative panels should be placed for 24 hours in the room where they'll be installed. This allows the panels to adjust to the moisture levels within the room and will help prevent future warping. Place the panels on their 8-foot edge and stack them out from the wall, inserting shims between the panels to expose all four sides to the air.

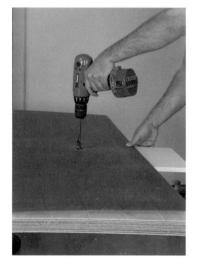

clean, and dry before installing panels. If the panels have a design pattern, make sure the pattern is placed in the same direction on all panels (flowers facing up, dark stripes on left side, etc.) when installing them. Cut panels to fit, and drill any holes for plumbing lines, etc., as needed (middle photo). To reduce chipping of the surface, cut panels face up with a fine-tooth handsaw, or face down with a fine-tooth portable jigsaw or circular saw. Then make sure to test the fit before applying adhesive, as shown in the bottom photo. On above-grade walls, leave 1/16" between panels to the left and right (along the 8-foot edge) and 1/8" at the top and bottom of the panels. For walls below grade, increase the top and bottom gap to 1/4"; use shims to create the correct spacing.

Cut panel as needed and test the fit. Tileboard is designed for applying directly to the wall surface; do not apply panels to furring strips or studs, as the panels will bow and warp. Make sure that all wall surfaces are firm,

Apply adhesive to the panel.
Use a high-quality, solvent-based trowel-grade tileboard or construction adhesive. Don't use water-

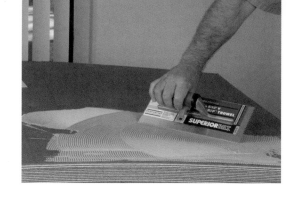

based adhesive, as it doesn't work well. With a 3/16" notched trowel held at a 45-degree angle, thoroughly cover the back of the wall panel with the adhesive, as shown in the top photo. Before attaching the panel to the wall, wait 5 to 10 minutes to allow excess solvents to evaporate. Adhesives should be tacky but not dry.

Apply the adhesive to wall. Use a flat trowel, and apply a thin layer to the wall area you will be covering with the panels, as shown in the bottom left photo.

Press the panels in place. Place the panel on the wall and press it firmly in place, as shown in the bottom right photo. A laminate roller does a good job of pressing the tileboard firmly into the wall to ensure a strong bond. Immediately wipe off any excess adhesive on the surface with mineral spirits (don't use lacquer thinner). Repeat this procedure for the remaining panels. Allow the adhesive to dry overnight.

Caulk the joints. The last thing to do is to fill in the gaps between the panels, as shown in the middle photo. Use 100% silicone caulk and apply it between the seams, to the edges around the panels, and around and behind all fixtures. To get straight and even caulk lines, apply painter's tape along panel edges and openings. Remove the tape as soon as caulking is complete.

Adding a Ramp

In the perfect accessible home, there wouldn't be any steps. Steps are barriers to many: anyone who isn't as strong or agile as they once were; anyone who uses a cane, walker, or wheelchair. Ramps are especially useful for providing access and circumventing exterior stairs. Ramps like the one illustrated in the drawing below can be built out of standard outdoor-rated lumber. The minimum slope recommended for a ramp is 1 in 12. A good ramp design should include a landing area that's large enough for a wheelchair to turn around in, and a railing on both sides to prevent falls. For a ramp to be solid, the support posts need to be anchored in concrete footings.

The Center for Universal Design, a division of the North Carolina State University School of Design, offers a booklet on wood ramp design that you can download for free from their website at: www.design.ncsu.edu/cud/pubs/wood_ramp.htm. This booklet describes how to add a ramp that both looks good and works well.

PRE-MADE RAMPS

■ When ramps aren't feasible but you still need a transition to move safely from one flooring height to another, consider a pre-made ramp like the one shown in the photo above. This unit, called the "EZ-Access Threshold Ramp," is made by North Coast Medical, Inc.; it's available in their print catalog ("Functional Solutions"), or at www.beabletodo.com. Designed to bridge most standard and sliding-door entries, this ramp lets wheelchairs and scooters navigate easily. The surface is non-skid and supports up to 600 pounds.

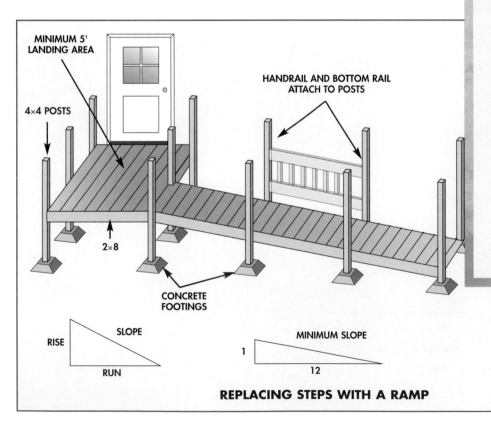

MINIMUM 5' LANDING AREA

4×4 POSTS

2×8

CONCRETE FOOTINGS

HANDRAIL AND BOTTOM RAIL ATTACH TO POSTS

RISE — SLOPE — RUN

MINIMUM SLOPE — 1 — 12

REPLACING STEPS WITH A RAMP

Adding a Berm

Whenever possible, berms should be used in place of steps or ramps. A berm is a sloped path made of soil or concrete that creates a smooth transition between different levels, as illustrated in the drawing at right. Because the surface of the berm is smooth, berms are easier to travel over than ramps for those walking, walking with a cane or walker, or seated in a wheelchair. If possible, a gradual slope of 1 in 20 should be used.

The construction of a berm is best left to a licensed landscaping contractor or other professional who deals with moving earth (like an excavation company or concrete contractor). That's because it takes knowledge and skill to create a berm with a rock-solid foundation that won't move or crack as the seasons change. It's also a good idea to create a protective edge along the berm, such as a hedge or railing, to prevent trips.

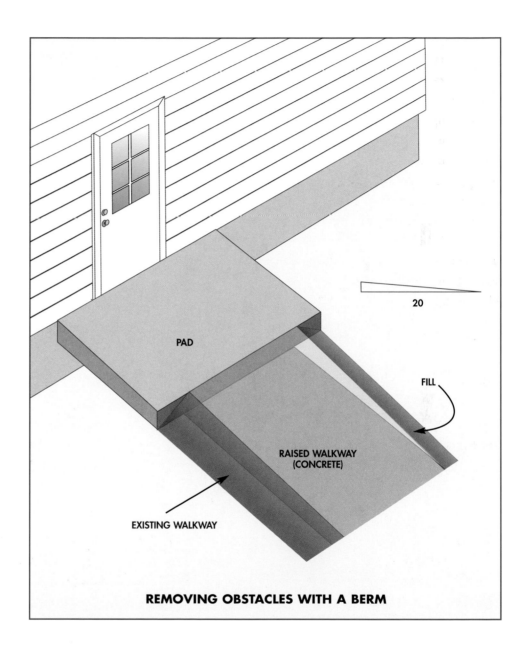

20

PAD

FILL

RAISED WALKWAY
(CONCRETE)

EXISTING WALKWAY

REMOVING OBSTACLES WITH A BERM

7

WINDOWS & DOORS

The features that make doors and windows suitable for an accessible home are the same ones that everyone appreciates. Doors need to be at least 36" wide (wider if possible), to allow plenty of room for those walking, unaided or with a cane or walker, or seated in a wheelchair. Of course, doors also need to be easy to open and close. How often have you struggled to open a stubborn double-hung window? That's why casement (crank) windows are preferred—they're easier to operate, whether you're sitting or standing.

In this chapter, we'll show you how to frame a new opening for a wider door, how to install a wider door, and how to make it easy to operate by installing a lever-style lockset. And, we'll show you how to increase door security with a deadbolt and peephole, and how to install accessible, mature-friendly pocket doors and casement windows.

Framing a Door

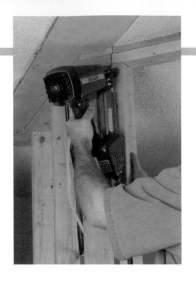

TOOLS

- Air nailer (optional)
- Tape measure and level
- Circular or miter saw
- Framing square
- Chalk line
- Hammer and nail set
- Driver/drill and bits
- Utility knife

To add a door to a wall, or to install a wider door, you'll need to frame a rough opening. Stud placement is critical here for the door to fit properly. In most cases, the rough opening should be 1/2" to 1" wider and taller than the unit you're installing (consult the manufacturer's instruction sheet for the recommended gap). This extra space allows you to adjust the unit for level and plumb with shims. In no case should you frame the opening for a wider gap. If you do, the fasteners you use to secure the door may penetrate only into the shims and not the jack or trimmer studs.

Install the king studs. Whenever possible, use an existing wall stud as one of the two king studs that define a rough opening. To locate the second king stud, you'll need to do a little math. Say, for instance, you're installing a 36"-wide door. Add 2" to this

for the two 1/2"-thick jambs and 1" for clearance—this means your jack studs need to be 38" apart. Now add 3" to this (for the two jack studs) and your second king stud needs to be 41" away from the first. Measure over the correct distance, cut a king stud to length, and toenail it to the top and bottom plates, as shown in the top photo.

ROUGH OPENING FOR A TYPICAL DOOR

The lighter arrows in the bottom drawing identify the finished opening of a door. The darker arrows show the rough opening. The framing members you'll need to install are: the king studs first, the jack or trimmer studs, and the header. Note that there's a gap at the bottom of the door for the threshold that may be installed later, or may come as part of the unit if it's a pre-hung door.

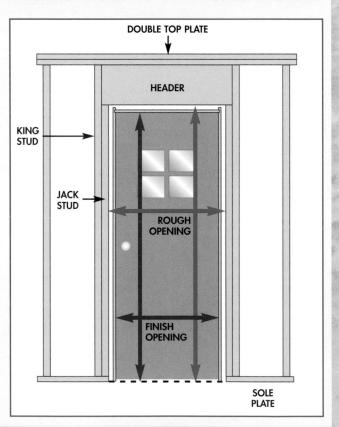

DOUBLE TOP PLATE

HEADER

KING STUD

JACK STUD

ROUGH OPENING

FINISH OPENING

SOLE PLATE

Install the jack studs. Next, cut two jack studs to length; these are usually 80" (standard door height). If your bottom plate extends out past the king studs and the jack studs will sit on top of these, subtract the thickness of the bottom plate (1 1/2") and cut the jack studs 78 1/2". Face-nail one of these to each of the king studs, as shown in the top left photo. It's a good idea now to re-measure the width of the opening and the actual width of the door to make sure it will fit in the rough opening.

Build the header. Headers are used to span the tops of doors and are designed to bear the weight of the wall studs that must be removed to make the door opening. The header is supported by jack studs, often called trimmer studs or vertical trimmers. These run alongside and are fastened to the king studs. Cripple studs connect the header to the top plate. With the jack and king studs in place, you can build the header. Note: If the wall you're working on is a load-bearing wall, consult your local building code for recommended header sizes. If you're working on a partition wall, measure the span between the king studs and cut a pair of 2×6's or 2×8's to this length. Since the combined thickness of the two 2-by pieces is only 3", a piece of 1/2" plywood or 1/2" plywood spacers are sandwiched in between the 2-bys to create a 3 1/2"-thick header.

Stack the header parts together with the ends flush and screw or nail them together, as shown in the middle left photo.

Install the header. Once you've built the header, lift it up and set it on top of the jack studs; if you measured and cut with precision, this should be a nice, snug fit. Adjust the header until its face is flush with the front and back edges of the king studs. Then secure the header by driving nails or screws through the king studs and into the ends of the header, as shown in the top right photo.

Add the cripple studs. Finally, you'll likely need to install cripple studs between the header and top plate. Measure the distance between the two, and cut short cripple studs to length. Face-nail one to each king stud, and then space the remaining cripple studs 16" on center; toenail them to the header and top plate, as shown in the bottom right photo. Note: With the door opening framed, it's now safe to remove any temporary supports that you may have installed (see page 115 for more on temporary supports).

Installing a Pre-Hung Door

TOOLS

- Hammer and nail set
- Caulking gun
- Screwdriver
- Level
- Driver/drill and bits
- Utility knife
- Combination square
- Handsaw and miter box or miter saw

The impact of a wider door can literally open up new possibilities for the accessible and mature-friendly home. All doors should be a minimum of 36" wide, wider if possible. With the advent of pre-hung doors, installing a new door is within the realm of the average DIYer. Hanging a new door is the easy part; the tough part is framing a wider opening for the door; see pages 130–131 for step-by-step directions on how to do this.

Insert door in opening. To hang a pre-hung door, start by removing the packing materials from the new door. Place the door in the opening to check the fit, as shown in the middle photo. If the door fits, check to make sure there's sufficient clearance between the jambs and framing for the shims that you'll use later to level the door.

HANDEDNESS OF DOORS

■ Here's how to tell if you want a right-handed or a left-handed door. For doors that swing in, look at the door from the outside of the home. If the hinges are on the left side, it's a left-handed swing-in door; on the right, and it's a right-handed swing-in door. If the door swings toward you looking at it from the outside of the home and the hinges are on the left side, it's a left-handed swing-out door; on the right, and it's a right-handed swing-out door.

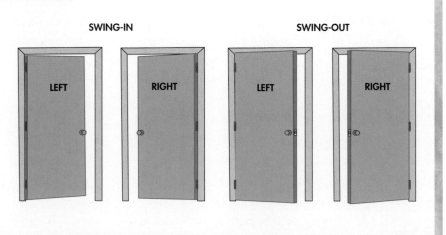

Shim and level. With the door positioned roughly in the opening, the next step is to add shims to level and plumb the door. Start by inserting shims behind each of the three hinges, behind the opening for the plunger for the door lockset, and at the top and bottom of the latch-side jamb. Also insert pairs of shims at the center and both ends of the head jamb. Insert the shims in pairs of opposing wedges, and adjust them in and out until they solidly fill the gap between the jamb and the framing members. Now hold a level up against one of the side jambs and check it for plumb. Adjust the position of the shims until the jamb is plumb, as shown in the top photo. Then move to the other side jamb and repeat the process. Finally, hold your level up against the head jamb to make sure it's level. If any of these are off, the door won't open or close properly. Take your time here and double-check everything once more before proceeding to the next step.

Secure the hinge-side jamb. When you're satisfied that the door is level and plumb, you can secure it to the hinge-side jamb. Your best bet here is a 2 1/2"- to 3"-long casing nail; use galvanized nails for exterior doors. Make sure to drive the nail through the hinge jamb only where the shims are. The idea here is to drive the nail though the jamb and the shims into the framing members, as shown in the middle photo. This way the jamb will be fully supported. As you nail the jamb in place, check for plumb again with a level and adjust the shims as necessary.

Drive screws through hinges. Most pre-hung doors come with three long hinge screws that are designed to pull the hinge-side jamb firmly into the framing members. The door hinges may or may not have an empty hole waiting for these. If not, you'll need to remove one screw from each jamb hinge and replace it with a longer screw, as shown in the bottom photo. If your door didn't come with these, use 3"-long galvanized deck screws and drive one into each hinge plate.

Secure the lockset jamb. Once you've secured the hinge-side jamb, turn your attention to the lockset jamb. Here again, you'll want to drive nails through the jamb only where the shims are located, as shown in the top photo. When you've secured both jambs and have double-checked that they are level and plumb, drive the nail heads below the surface with a nail set and hammer.

Cut off the shims. On both sides of the door, cut off any protruding shims with a sharp utility knife, as shown in the middle photo. Score the shim at the jamb and then snap it off.

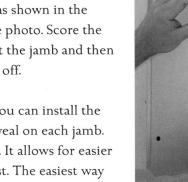

Attach the trim. With the shims out of the way, you can install the door trim. To install miter trim, start by marking the reveal on each jamb. A reveal is a slight offset between the trim and the jamb. It allows for easier installation and provides a shadow line for visual interest. The easiest way to mark this is to set the blade of a combination square so that it protrudes 1/8". Then place a pencil against the blade of the square, press the head of the square against the jamb, and run these around the perimeter to mark the reveal.

Once you've measured the trim pieces, you can cut them to length with a handsaw and a miter box, or a power miter saw. Position each piece one at a time so the inside edge is flush with the marked reveal line. Nail the trim to the jamb with finish nails spaced about 12" apart. Set the nail heads and fill the nail holes with putty. Sand smooth when dry, and paint the door and trim as desired. Finally, install the lockset of your choice (see pages 135–137) and test the operation of the door. If all went well, the door should open and close smoothly.

Installing Lever-Style Handsets

TOOLS

- Hammer and chisel (optional)
- Screwdriver

Now's the time to discard those old hard-to-grip doorknobs and upgrade your locksets to a mature-friendly, lever-style lockset like the one shown in the top photo.

The ease of installing a new lockset will depend on a couple of things. First, if you're simply replacing an old lockset and the new unit is sized similarly, it's just a matter of reversing the order of disassembly to install the new unit. As long as the hole sizes are the same, most new locksets let you

adjust the length of the plunger to compensate for differences in the offset—that is, the distance the large hole is from the edge of the door. If you insert the plunger and find that the stem holes (the holes through which the mounting screws pass) are centered in the hole, the plunger needs no adjustment.

LOCKING MECHANISMS

■ Not all lever-style locksets are the same. When shopping for new locksets, look for those that have easy-to-use locking mechanisms as described below. All the locksets we installed in our accessible home makeover are manufactured by Schlage (www.schlage.com).

The lever-style locksets showcased here, like Schlage's deadbolts (see page 138), feature all-metal locking mechanisms and lifetime mechanical warranties. What's more, they're all easy to install, with a three-piece assembly. The lever-style locksets are "field reversible" (nixing the need for handing), offer universal fit, and comply with the regulations from the ADA (Americans with Disabilities Act). Recognizing that more and more people want the easy use of a lever-style lockset, Schlage offers theirs in several styles and finishes.

Bad: The locking mechanism on this poorly designed lever-style handset is a tiny actuator that is gripped by pinching it. If this isn't difficult enough, you have to rotate the actuator to lock or unlock the handset.

Good: A more mature-friendly locking mechanism like the one on this Schlage lever-style handset is operated by pushing in a button. This is easy to do with a finger or even a knuckle.

Change plunger plates if necessary. With a quality lockset, the manufacturer will provide two different-shaped plates to attach to the plunger mechanism, as shown in the top photo; one plate is rectangular and the other has rounded corners. The rectangular plate is used for existing doors that have a square mortise. If you're installing the lockset in a new door, odds are that the mortise for the plunger mechanism will have rounded ends. That's because the mortise was milled with a round router bit. With two plates, you just pick the one that fits your mortise and snap it onto the plunger mechanism. If your lockset doesn't come with two plates, it'll likely come with just a rectangular plate. So in a new door you'll have to square up the corners of the mortise with a chisel so that it'll fit.

Install the plunger. With the correct plate on the plunger mechanism (or with the mortise modified as needed), you can install the plunger mechanism in the edge of the door. Press the plunger mechanism all the way in. Then drill two pilot holes to accept the mounting screws provided and install these with a screwdriver, as shown in the middle photo. Note: If you're replacing a lockset and will be using the existing holes, consider inserting wood toothpicks into the existing holes to give the screw threads something to bite into.

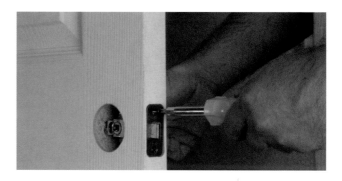

HANDSET ANATOMY

■ The typical handset consists of three main parts: a two-section lever assembly and a plunger, as illustrated in the drawing below. One half of the lever assembly usually houses the actuator—that is, a metal bar or tube that passes through the plunger into the opposite handle assembly. When either lever is operated, it rotates the actuator to pull the plunger in the latch in, allowing the door to open. The plunger mates up with a strike plate mortised into the doorjamb.

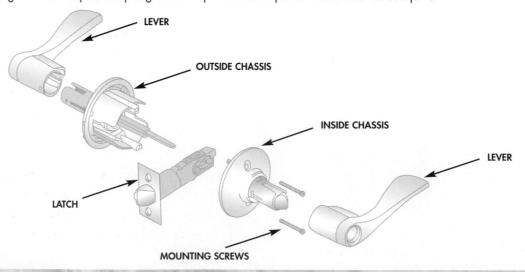

LEVER

OUTSIDE CHASSIS

INSIDE CHASSIS

LEVER

LATCH

MOUNTING SCREWS

Install one half of the handset. Now that the plunger mechanism is in place, you can begin installing the two halves of the lockset. Start by inserting the half that contains the actuator that passes through the plunger mechanism. In most cases, it's keyed to fit only one way. Insert the tip of the actuator in the hole in the plunger mechanism. Push the lever in until it butts up against the face of the door, as shown in the top photo. Check the operation now by turning the handle—the plunger should go in and out as you turn.

Attach the second half of lockset. Next, install the second half of the lockset. Align the actuator with the hole in the lever assembly and push until it butts up against the face of the door. Now insert the screws in the holes in the lever assembly so they pass through the stem holes in the plunger and into the second half of the lockset. Tighten these with a screwdriver (as shown in the middle photo), and check the operation of the plunger again.

Install the strike plate. With the lockset in place, you can install the strike plate in the doorjamb. For a replacement lockset, position the new strike plate where the existing one was. To locate a strike plate on a new door, try this simple trick: Rub a little lipstick or crayon on the plunger, then close the door. The lipstick will leave a mark on the doorjamb exactly where you'll need to locate the strike plate. If necessary, drill a clearance hole for the plunger. Then drill pilot holes for the strike plate and secure it with the screws provided, as shown in the bottom photo.

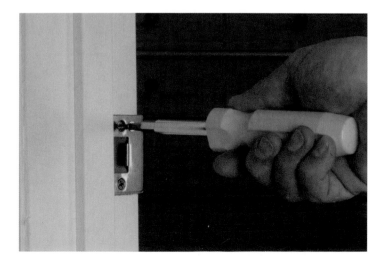

Door Security

TOOLS

- Hammer and chisel
- Drill and bits
- Awl
- Screwdriver

Security becomes increasingly important as we age. Reductions in vision, hearing, and mobility may make us feel more vulnerable, along with the solo living status of many older Americans. You can enhance your safety by making an exterior door more secure: Two ways to do this are by adding a deadbolt and installing a peephole. A deadbolt adds an extra level of security to a door, while a peephole lets you see who's there before you open the door.

The deadbolt we installed here is manufactured by Schlage (www.schlage.com) and features a large, easy-to-operate deadbolt throw. Although most new pre-hung doors are pre-bored for a lockset, it's rare to find any that are bored for a deadbolt. If part of your makeover calls for a new exterior door and you're ordering it from a home center or lumberyard, check to see whether they'll bore the door for a deadbolt as well as the lockset. If not, you'll need to drill these holes yourself; see below.

Locate the mounting holes. Deadbolts are usually installed 3" above the center of a locket. Quality deadbolts include a template that makes laying out the necessary mounting holes easy. To use the template, fold it at the appropriate line to match the thickness of your door. Measure up the recommended distance and affix the template to the door temporarily with masking tape, as shown in the middle photo. Then use an awl to poke through the template to mark the hole locations: one on the edge for the plunger mechanism, and one on the door face for the deadbolt.

Drill the mounting holes. Remove the template and, using the recommended drill bits, drill the two holes—first the plunger hole (bottom photo) and then the deadbolt hole (photo at right). When drilling the deadbolt hole, stop halfway and then drill in from the other face. This will prevent the drill bit from splintering the face of the door as it breaks through the other side.

DEADBOLT ANATOMY

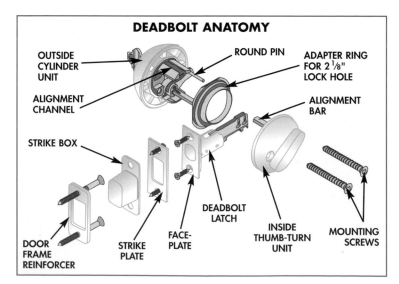

OUTSIDE CYLINDER UNIT

ROUND PIN

ADAPTER RING FOR 2 1/8" LOCK HOLE

ALIGNMENT CHANNEL

ALIGNMENT BAR

STRIKE BOX

DEADBOLT LATCH

INSIDE THUMB-TURN UNIT

MOUNTING SCREWS

DOOR FRAME REINFORCER

STRIKE PLATE

FACE-PLATE

Install plunger. In most cases, you'll need to cut a mortise in the door edge for the plunger faceplate. To do this, push the plunger in until its faceplate butts up against the edge and trace around it with a pencil. Then remove about 1/8" of material inside the marked lines with a chisel. With the mortise cut, press the plunger all the way in. Then drill two pilot holes to accept the mounting screws provided and drive these in, as shown in the top photo.

Install the deadbolt. With the plunger mechanism in place, install the two halves of the deadbolt. Start by inserting the half that contains

the actuator that passes through the plunger mechanism. In most cases, it's keyed to fit only one way. Insert the tip of the actuator in the hole in the plunger mechanism and push in until it butts up against the face of the door. Then install the mating half. Align the actuator with the hole in the remaining deadbolt half and push until it butts up against the face of the door. Now insert the screws in the holes in the deadbolt so they pass through the stem holes in the plunger and into the second half of the deadbolt. Tighten these with a screwdriver (as shown in the top right photo), and check the operation of the plunger. Finally, drill a hole for the strike plate and install it in the doorjamb.

INSTALLING A PEEPHOLE

■ Someone's knocking on your door and you don't know who it is: That's a potentially unsafe situation. The good news is that you can totally prevent this by installing peepholes in your exterior doors. When shopping for a peephole, look for the full-view type that shows outside from the ground up—this prevents an unwanted guest from hiding low in front of the door so you can't see him.

Peepholes are a breeze to install; they consist of two parts that pass through a hole in the door and are threaded together.

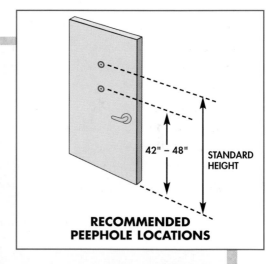

42" – 48"

STANDARD HEIGHT

RECOMMENDED PEEPHOLE LOCATIONS

Locate the peephole. The simplest way to locate a peephole is to stand in front of the door and hold the peephole out so it's level with your eyes; then make a mark at this height. Alternatively, see the drawing above right.

Drill the mounting hole. Using the recommended bit, drill a hole through the door at the location you just marked.

Install the peephole. Pass one half of the peephole through each side of the door and thread the parts together until tight.

Installing a Pocket Door

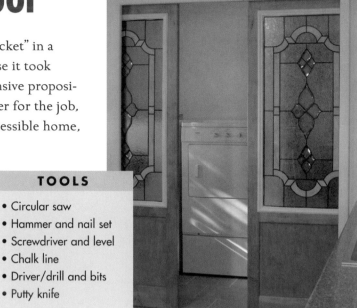

In the past, pocket doors, which slide in and out of a "pocket" in a wall, were common only in pricier homes. That's because it took money to afford pocket doors: Installation was an expensive proposition. You needed an experienced carpenter or trim carpenter for the job, and for the most part, it was a custom project. In today's accessible home, pocket doors make sense: They don't take up any floor space, so they're perfect for tight areas. And now, even a tight budget has room for a pocket door. The folks at Johnson Hardware (www.johnsonhardware.com) have come up with a unique pocket door hardware kit. It lets you use an existing door (or a new one) and install it in the average interior wall constructed from 2×4 lumber—no additional wall thickness is required, as it was in the past. You can install one of these in any 2×4 wall as long as there are no utilities in the wall: electrical, plumbing, or gas lines (Johnson Hardware also offers pocket door kits for 2×6 walls).

A pocket door kit consists of two pairs of split jambs that protect the door and provide a means for fastening on the wall covering; a frame header; and mounting hardware that accepts a pair of track wheel assemblies, as illustrated in the bottom drawing. The door attaches to these wheels to slide back and forth, as illustrated in the drawing below. The split jambs are wood strips partially encased in steel for strength, with slots cut in them so you can attach trim. At the top, they attach to the frame header; at the bottom they clip onto a pair of floor plates that are screwed to the floor.

TOOLS

- Circular saw
- Hammer and nail set
- Screwdriver and level
- Chalk line
- Driver/drill and bits
- Putty knife

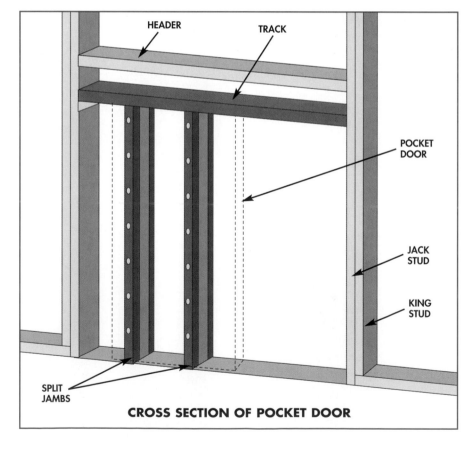

CROSS SECTION OF POCKET DOOR

Build the frame. The first step to installing a pocket door is to remove the existing wall covering. If the wall is load-bearing, install supports before removing any studs (see page 115). Then remove the necessary studs and build a frame, following the manufacturer's directions. For load-bearing walls, check with your local building inspector for the size header you'll need to install. Install the king and jack studs, then the header as shown in the top photo. Measure, cut, and install cripple studs as required. For more on door framing, see page 130.

Attach the frame header. With the frame complete, the next step is to install the frame header. This hooks onto a pair of metal brackets that attach to the frame (inset). Locate the brackets per the manufacturer's instructions and then set the header frame in place, as shown in the middle right photo. Check to make sure the frame header is level, and secure the brackets to the frame.

Attach the split jambs. Now you can attach the split jambs. Snap a chalk line on the floor, even with the frame studs, to locate the floor plate that secures the split jambs to the floor. Slip the slots in the ends of the split jambs onto the fingers of the floor plates; butt the top of the split jamb onto the frame header as directed. Nail the tops of the split jambs into the frame header as shown in the bottom photo. After checking to make sure they're plumb and level, secure the floor plates to the floor with screws. Repeat for the other pair of split jambs, positioning them about midway in the pocket opening.

SMOOTH SLIDING

■ The track wheel assemblies fit into a metal channel on the frame header. They accept a pair of door plates that attach to the door. For even smoother operation, ball-bearing wheel assemblies can be purchased to replace the standard wheels. Not only are these quieter and smoother, but they'll also last longer, as the sealed bearings are virtually impervious to wear and tear.

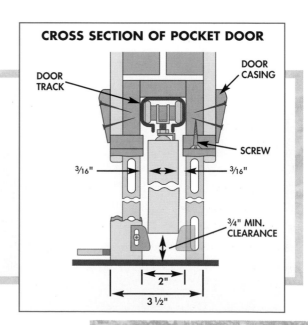

CROSS SECTION OF POCKET DOOR

DOOR TRACK

DOOR CASING

SCREW

3/16" 3/16"

3/4" MIN. CLEARANCE

2"

3 1/2"

Install the wall covering. Now you can add the wall covering. Cut and install drywall to cover the frame. Screw the drywall to the exposed wood strip portions of the split jambs and the frame you built, as shown in the top photo. Apply tape and drywall compound as explained on pages 120–121.

Hang the door and add the stops. To hang the door, start by attaching the door plates to the top of the door as directed, as shown in the middle right photo. Slip the track wheel assemblies onto the frame header and then lift the door into position. Posts on the door plates slip into grooves in the track wheel assemblies. A nylon stop strip is then pivoted over to lock the door in place. With the door in place, you can install the stop. Each stop slips into one end of the track and contains a rubber bumper as a cushion. Slide the stop to the desired point and tighten it in place as shown in the inset photo at right.

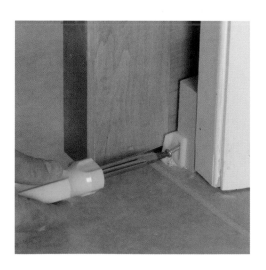

Finishing touches. Start by covering the exposed ends of the pocket door with 1-by stock. Johnson Hardware sells a jamb kit that makes installation a snap. Then cut and install casing around the door frame and set and fill all nail holes. Paint the door and trim (if desired). Install the plastic guides at the bottom of the jamb that keep the door bottom from swaying as it's opened and closed (you may need to attach the guides to wood scraps to extend them, as shown in the photo at right). Finally, the posts on the top plates can be adjusted to raise or lower each end of the door independently to level it (photo at left).

INSTALLING GLASS INSERTS

■ Most interior doors are a solid slab. Most are also, well, pretty boring. A glass insert like the one shown in the top photo is a perfect way to dress up a door while also allowing light to filter from room to room. The insert shown here and featured in our accessible kitchen makeover (page 71) is manufactured by ODL (www.odl.com). ODL makes an amazing array of glass inserts (and glass block, too) in shapes, sizes, and styles to fit almost any room, or an exterior door. An opening has to be cut in an interior door for the insert, but this is easily accomplished by following the manufacturer's directions.

Place the insert in the door opening. With the opening cut, you can install the glass insert either with the door resting on a pair of sawhorses or after the door has been hung, as shown here. Start by separating the two halves of the insert—the insert itself and the keeper frame that holds it in place. Carefully position the insert in the door opening, as shown. Align the insert so it's centered in the door opening from side to side and from top to bottom. You may find that shims are helpful here to keep the insert from shifting.

Add the mounting frame. While holding the insert in place, have a helper position the keeper frame on the other side of the door so the holes in the keeper frame align with those in the glass insert, as shown in the near right bottom photo.

Secure the frame to the insert. To secure the insert in the door opening, drive screws in through the keeper frame and into the holes in the glass insert, as shown in the far right bottom photo. When all the screws are in place, insert the plastic covers that conceal the screw heads.

Installing a Casement Window

TOOLS

- Tape measure and level
- Pry bar and putty knife
- Hammer and nail set
- Screwdriver (optional)
- Caulking gun
- Air nailer (optional)
- Utility knife
- Reciprocating saw (optional)
- Combination square
- Handsaw and miter box or miter saw

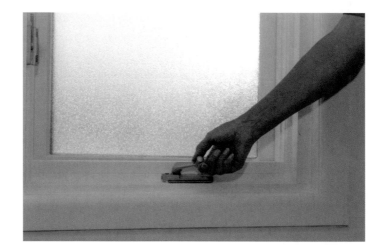

Of all the window types available, casement windows are the most mature-friendly. Actually, they're just the most people-friendly because they open and close by turning a crank. This is easy to do while standing or sitting— much easier than operating a sliding or standard double-hung window. Casement windows can be ordered from home centers, lumberyards, and specialty window stores. Make sure to bring accurate measurements of your existing window or windows when ordering replacements. Note: Since window sizes vary tremendously, you may need to alter the wall framing to accept the new window. Consult a licensed contractor, carpenter, or window specialist if this is necessary.

Remove the existing trim. To replace an existing window with a casement window, start by removing the trim on both sides of the window. For situations where you know you won't be reusing the existing trim, you can remove the trim quickly with a pry bar, as shown in the bottom photo.

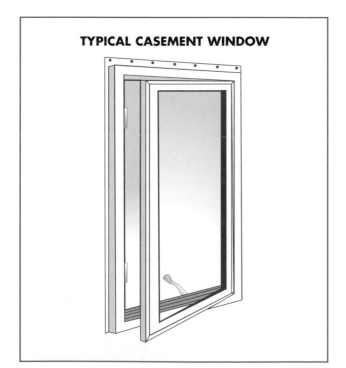

TYPICAL CASEMENT WINDOW

Remove the old window. How you free a window from the surrounding framing will depend on how it was installed. If the window is screwed in place (as shown in the inset photo below), simply remove the screws. Most windows, though, are held in place with nails driven through the jambs and into the framing. The quickest way to release a window installed with nails is to cut through the nails; a reciprocating saw fitted with a demolition blade works best for this. Insert the blade between the jamb and the framing and cut all the nails. At this point the window should be free and ready to be removed. For larger windows, have a helper on hand as you pull

it out of the rough opening, as shown in the top left photo.

Insert the new casement window. If you measured correctly and the opening is the correct size, the new window should slide in easily (bottom photo). You should have about 1/2" to 1" combined clearance between the sides of the new window and the jamb. This space

allows you to slip in shims and level the window; see below.

Shim and secure the window. In order for the new window to operate without binding, it's important that the window be installed level and plumb. Check for this with a level on the sides, top, and bottom. Insert pairs of shims as needed in the gaps between the sides of the new window and the jambs. Slide the shims back and forth and in and out until the window is level and plumb. Then secure the window to the jamb with casing nails, as shown in the top right photo. Cut off any protruding shims with a sharp utility knife.

Add the trim. Finally, you can add the trim. To install mitered trim, start by marking the reveal on each jamb. The easiest way to mark this is to set the blade of a

combination square so it protrudes 1/8". Then place a pencil against the blade of the square, press the head of the square against the jamb, and run these around the perimeter to mark the reveal. Once you've measured the trim pieces, cut them to length and attach them to the jamb and framing members as shown in the bottom right photo. Fill all nail holes with putty, caulk around the trim to seal any gaps, and apply the finish of your choice.

8

PLUMBING

Many elements large and small make up successful aging in place, and the same thing applies to plumbing projects that boost comfort and safety. Since personal hygiene is such a key part of independent living, plumbing upgrades can make a big difference in everyday life. Your accessible bath makeover might be as simple as replacing a tough-to-operate faucet with an easy-to-use lever-style version. Or, you might ditch that inaccessible bathtub for a leading-edge walk-in model. Each of the projects in this chapter is all about making daily hygiene easier.

We'll show you how to remove an old vanity, toilet, and shower to make room for more accessible and mature-friendly versions like wall-mount sinks, raised-height toilets, walk-in bathtubs, and low-threshold showers. And any updated bathroom can benefit from the addition of a grab bar or two for better support while sitting or standing up or down.

Removing a Vanity

TOOLS

- Screwdriver or nutdriver
- Slip-joint pliers
- Adjustable wrench
- Putty knife

Removing a vanity is a pretty straightforward job. It is, after all, a single cabinet. But there's a complication: the plumbing. You need to disconnect the supply and waste lines running to the sink and faucet. This in itself isn't that difficult, either, except you're usually working in cramped quarters with insufficient light. That's why the first step to removing a vanity is removing the doors.

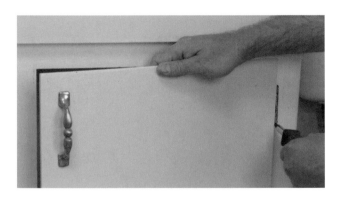

Prepare the cabinet for removal.
Removing the doors to a vanity cabinet does three things: It makes a restrictive space less restrictive, it lets in light, and it lessens the weight of the vanity. Remove the screws holding the door hinges to the cabinet and set the door or doors aside, as shown in the above photo. Next, turn off the water at the shut-off valves for both the hot and cold water lines (inset photo).

Disconnect the waste and supply lines.
Once the doors are out of the way, you can disconnect the plumbing to the sink and faucet. It's easiest to start with the waste line, as this is in front of the supply lines. Loosen the nut holding the trap in place; have a bucket and towel handy to catch the inevitable water flow, as shown in the top right photo. After you remove the trap, temporarily plug the waste line with a rag to prevent sewer gas from leaking into your house. Next, disconnect the faucet lines running to the shut-off valves (inset photo).

Remove the countertop screws. To further lessen the weight of the vanity, it's best to remove the countertop and sink/faucet as a single unit. Most vanity tops are attached via mounting screws underneath that pass through metal brackets or wood cleats to the top inside edges of the vanity. Remove the screws with a screwdriver or nutdriver, as shown in the photo at left.

Loosen the caulk at the backsplash. To prevent water from leaking behind the vanity, most backsplashes have been caulked to seal any gaps between the wall and the backsplash.

Take the time to sever this bond by running a putty knife along the back edge, as shown in the top left photo. Skipping this step will likely lead to wall damage when the countertop is removed. You'd be surprised how strong a bond aged caulk can create—strong enough to tear the top layer of paper right off your drywall.

Lift off the counter. With the caulk bond severed, you can safely lift off the countertop and set it aside, as shown in the bottom left photo. Depending on whether you left the faucet supply piping connected to the faucet, you may need to lift the countertop quite high to clear the sides of the vanity. Whenever possible, have a helper on hand for this job.

Pull out the vanity. All that's left is to pull out the vanity. Depending on how it was installed, you may have to remove the cove base or base trim. This is necessary only if you need to expose screws driven through the base of the cabinet into the floor to secure it. Otherwise, locate and remove the screws or nails in the backs of the cabinets that secure them to the wall (inset photo below). You should now be able to lift and pull the vanity away from the wall, as shown in the middle photo. If you encounter resistance, you've probably missed a mounting screw. Locate and remove the screw or screws and try again—in older cabinets, these may be hard to find, as installers often covered screw heads with putty to make them less visible.

Removing a Toilet

TOOLS

- Adjustable wrench
- Screwdriver
- Bucket and sponge
- Hacksaw (optional)
- Putty knife

One of the simplest plumbing projects for making a bathroom aging-friendly is to replace a standard toilet with a raised-height toilet, as described on pages 159–161. To do this, naturally, you'll need to remove the old one first. Although this isn't one of the most pleasant tasks of a makeover, it's pretty simple. Just make sure to have plenty of towels and rags on hand to clean up water spills, and a helper to remove and dispose of the old toilet (even when separated into two parts, toilets are surprisingly heavy).

Shut off and disconnect the water line.

To remove a toilet, begin by shutting off water to the toilet and emptying the tank completely. Flush the toilet and leave the handle depressed to empty as much water out of the tank as possible. Then sop up the remaining water with a sponge. Next, use an adjustable wrench to loosen the supply line to the toilet. Then unhook this line from the shut-off valve, as shown in the bottom left photo.

Bail out any standing water. Before you remove the bowl, take the time to bail out as much water as possible from the bowl, as shown in the top photo. This will help prevent spills when you lift up and carry away the bowl later.

Remove the tank. Although it's not absolutely necessary, it's always a good idea to remove the tank from the bowl to lessen the weight of the toilet. (The weight of the bowl alone is enough to strain most backs.) The tank is held in place by a set of screws inside at the bottom. These screws pass through rubber washers and into a ledge of the bowl, where they're held in place with nuts. Hold each nut securely and loosen the bolt with a screwdriver. Then lift the tank off the bowl, as shown in the bottom right photo.

Remove the mounting nuts. Next, pry off the decorative caps at the base of the toilet that cover the closet bolts and mounting nuts. (Closet bolts are sometimes referred to as "Johnny" bolts.) The nuts that thread onto the closet bolts have a well-deserved reputation for not coming off easily. Try loosening them with an adjustable wrench, as shown in the top photo. If they don't come off easily, apply some penetrating oil and allow it to soak 15 minutes before trying again. If that doesn't do the trick, you'll have to cut the nuts off with a hacksaw.

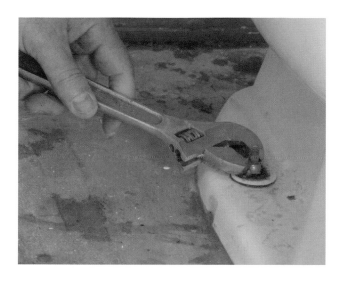

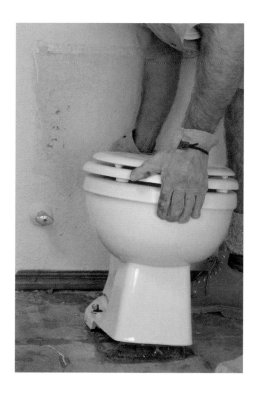

Lift off the toilet. Once the mounting nuts have been removed, lift the toilet gently off the floor, as shown in the middle photo. Since there's sure to be water still remaining in the integral trap, be careful as you move it about; empty this water into a bucket and set the toilet on its side on an old towel. If you find that the toilet won't come up easily, try rocking it gently from side to side to break the old seal.

Plug the opening and clean the flange. As soon as you've set the toilet aside, plug the drain opening with a rag to prevent sewer gas from rising up into the house. Make sure the rag is large enough that it can't accidentally fall down into the waste line. Remove the old closet bolts from the closet flange and set them aside if you're planning to reuse them. Finally, use a putty knife to scrape away the old wax ring from both the closet flange and the floor, as shown in the bottom photo. This usually looks more vile than it is, as the natural color of most wax rings is brown. Wipe away any remaining wax with a clean, soft rag. If you'll be installing new flooring over the old floor, take the time to thoroughly remove all wax on the floor: The old wax can prevent the new flooring from bonding well to the old floor.

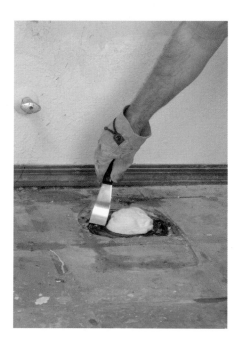

Removing a Tub or Shower

TOOLS

- Utility knife
- Pry bar
- Screwdriver (optional)
- Circular saw or reciprocating saw
- Hammer

When a bathroom makeover calls for a new shower or bathtub, naturally, you'll first need to remove the old unit. How you do this will depend on what the tub or shower is made of. If you're lucky, the unit will be made of fiberglass, which can be cut into sections for easy removal (see below). But if your old tub is cast iron, consider bringing in a licensed plumber to remove it. In most cases, this will involve breaking the tub in two and then lifting it out in pieces. Even half a cast-iron tub is more than most people's backs can handle—this is one of those jobs best left to a professional.

Remove the drywall. To remove a fiberglass tub or shower enclosure, the first thing to do is to remove the surrounding drywall to expose the fasteners that secure the tub or surround to the wall studs. Cut the drywall into manageable pieces with a utility knife and pry the pieces off the studs with a

pry bar. Pull them off the wall as shown in the bottom left photo, and set them aside for disposal. Make sure to wear gloves to protect your hands and a dust mask to protect your lungs from the inevitable construction dust.

Remove the mounting fasteners. With the fasteners exposed, you can remove them with a pry bar or screwdriver, as shown in the top photo. You should find a fastener at every stud location and spaced about every 8" to 10" along the vertical flange of the tub or surround.

Remove cover plates and showerhead. Next, you'll need to remove the shower or tub control handles and any cover plates or escutcheons that cover the valves. On bathtubs, remove the spout; and on showers, unscrew the showerhead, as shown in the bottom right photo.

Cut through the sides and base. Since many fiberglass tub and shower enclosures are single-piece units and were installed before the rest of the bathroom was framed, they can't be removed in a single piece. This means they have to come out in pieces. Fiberglass cuts fairly easily, but this tends to create a lot of dust—and this dust is especially bad for your lungs. So before you cut, close in the bathroom area with a tarp, and don a dust mask and eye protection. We used a portable trim saw to cut the fiberglass, as shown in the top photo, but a reciprocating saw fitted with a short demolition blade also works well. The thing you have to be careful about is to not cut into plumbing or electrical lines in the walls. The easiest way to prevent this is to set your saw blade depth to just barely cut through the surface of the fiberglass. Make cuts near the base of the unit and near each corner; then cut the base in two.

Remove the sides. With a little luck, you'll be able to pull the side units out, as shown in the middle photo. If there are areas where you couldn't cut with the saw, you can break the fiberglass section free by hitting it near a cut line with a hammer. Make sure to wear gloves and a dust mask when handling these sections.

Pull out the base. Once all sides and the back have been removed, you can tackle the base. Start by removing the drain cap. Then insert a pry bar under the base and lift up. In some cases the base will have been set into thin-set mortar, and this step is necessary to break the bond. Lift up each section and set it aside for disposal, as shown in the bottom photo.

Installing a Lever-Style Faucet

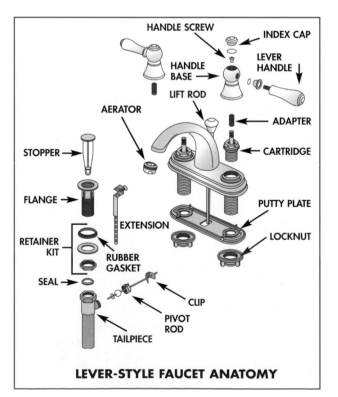

TOOLS

- Adjustable wrench
- Slip-joint pliers
- Basin wrench (optional)
- Plastic putty knife
- Screwdriver

A faucet with an easy-to-use handle or levers like the one shown in the top photo is the only way to go in an accessible bathroom. That's because you can operate the faucet without having to grasp and rotate knobs. We chose a center-set faucet from American Standard (www.americanstandard.com) because it's basically one piece and therefore is the simplest type of faucet to install. The valves on most center-set faucets are spaced on 4" centers. This is something to keep in mind when shopping for both a sink and a faucet. Many newer sinks have 8" on-center spacing and require the use of a widespread faucet.

If you're just replacing the faucet and not the sink, turn the water off and, with an adjustable wrench, loosen the nuts connecting the faucet supply lines to the shut-off valves, or main water lines. If you're not planning to remove the sink to install the new faucet, use a basin wrench to loosen the faucet-mounting nuts. Before you remove the old faucet, run the blade of a putty knife around its perimeter to sever the bond (old caulk or plumber's putty) between the faucet and sink. Once you've pulled out the old faucet, remove old putty or caulk from the sink so you'll get a good seal under the new faucet. Use a plastic putty knife to scrape away the bulk of the old sealant. Then clean the surface thoroughly with a soft rag and some denatured alcohol.

Install the faucet.

To install a center-set faucet, start by slipping the gasket provided onto the bottom of the faucet. Alternatively, do what many plumbers do—throw away the gasket and pack the cavities under the baseplate with plumber's putty. Next, slip the valves of the faucet through the holes in the sink. Thread the mounting nuts onto the valves, as shown in the top photo. Check to make sure

LEVER-STYLE FAUCET ANATOMY

(labels: HANDLE SCREW, INDEX CAP, HANDLE BASE, LEVER HANDLE, LIFT ROD, AERATOR, ADAPTER, CARTRIDGE, STOPPER, FLANGE, EXTENSION, PUTTY PLATE, RETAINER KIT, RUBBER GASKET, LOCKNUT, SEAL, CLIP, PIVOT ROD, TAILPIECE)

the faucet is centered on the sink, and tighten the nuts hand-tight. Then give them another quarter turn with a pair of slip-joint pliers or a basin wrench, as shown in the top left photo. If you packed the faucet cavity with plumber's putty, remove any squeeze-out with a plastic putty knife.

Attach the supply lines. If you're installing the faucet with the sink removed, it's easiest to connect one end of the supply tubes to the valves now. Start by wrapping a couple of turns of Teflon tape around the valve threads; then thread on the nuts and tighten them with an adjustable wrench. If you're working with the sink in place, use a basin wrench to tighten the mounting nuts.

Install the drain and pop-up mechanism.
Next, wrap a coil of plumber's putty around the drain flange and insert it through the drain opening in the sink. Thread this into the drain body; then, using a pair of slip-joint pliers, tighten the nut to push the rubber gasket up against the bottom of the drain opening. Wrap a few turns of Teflon tape around the tailpiece and screw it into the drain body. Insert the plunger through the drain flange into the drain body. Align the slot in the end of the plunger with the opening in the drain body for the pivot rod. Then insert the washer and pivot rod into the opening in the drain body so the end of the pivot rod passes through the slot in the end of the plunger, as shown in the top right photo. Slip the plastic nut over the open end of the pivot rod and thread this into the drain body. Tighten friction-tight and check the action of the plunger by

pivoting the rod up and down—the plunger should open and close as you do this.

To connect the pivot rod to the lift rod (also called the pop-up rod), start by sliding the lift rod through the opening in the faucet body. Then slip the extension rod over the lift rod and secure it with the thumbscrew on the end of the extension rod. Bend the extension rod as necessary so one of its holes aligns with the pivot rod. Connect the pivot rod to the extension with the spring clip provided. Check the plunger action by moving the lift rod up and down. Adjust the extension as necessary for smooth operation (inset photo above).

Connect lines and add handles. If you've installed the faucet with the sink removed, now install the sink. Then connect the open end of the supply tubes to the shut-off valves. Wrap the threads on the shut-off

valve with Teflon tape, thread on the tubes, and tighten the nuts with an adjustable wrench (inset photo below). Connect the tailpiece to the trap and existing waste line. Finally, install the

handles, as shown in the bottom photo. Remove the faucet's aerator, turn on the water, and flush the system. When the water runs clear, turn off the faucet and re-install the aerator.

A Wall-Mount Sink

TOOLS

- Electric drill and bits
- Screwdriver and level
- Socket wrench (optional)
- Adjustable wrench
- Slip-joint pliers
- Handsaw
- Hammer
- Air nailer (optional)
- Tubing cutter

One of the best ways to make a bathroom more accessible is to replace a vanity-mounted sink with a wall-mounted version. Instantly, the room will seem larger. You'll also gain more real floor space, which can make standing or sitting in front of the sink more comfortable. And dirt, dust, and hair will have fewer places to hide. But there is a drawback to a wall-mount sink. Because the weight of the sink must be borne by the wall, you'll need to add a support cleat to the framing—and this means removing the wall covering.

Wall-mount sinks attach to a wall in three different ways: They can be screwed directly to the wall or hang from a bracket, or both as illustrated in the drawing below. The American Standard sink shown here attaches directly to the wall via a pair of bolts that thread into the wall cleat.

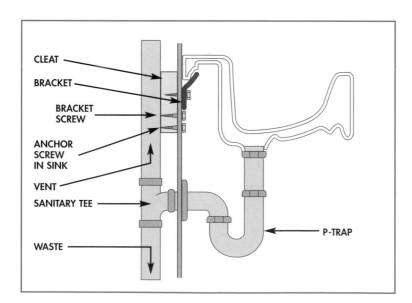

CLEAT
BRACKET
BRACKET SCREW
ANCHOR SCREW IN SINK
VENT
SANITARY TEE
WASTE
P-TRAP

Prepare the wall. If your old sink wasn't wall-mounted, you'll need to remove the wall covering, install a cleat, and replace the wall covering, as illustrated in the drawing at left. Consult the directions that came with your sink to locate the cleat. Measure up and cut partially through the wall studs (inset photo below). Knock out the waste and insert the recommended-size cleat. Attach the cleat to the wall studs with screws or nails, as shown in the middle photo. In some cases, you'll need to re-plumb the supply and waste lines before replacing the wall covering.

Install mounting bolts or bracket.

With the wall covering in place, measure up from the floor and mark the locations of the mounting bolts (main photo above). Drill the recommended-size holes and drive the hanger bolts through the wall covering and into the wall cleat, as shown in the inset photo above. If your wall-mount sink uses a bracket, install it now.

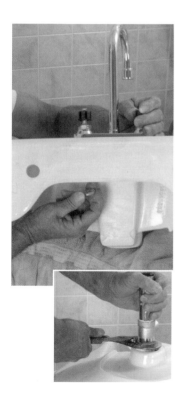

Install faucet and pop-up mechanism.

Before you attach a wall-mount sink to the wall, it's best to install the faucet and pop-up mechanism. Even though there's no vanity to crawl into for hooking up the faucet, it's easier to install the faucet now when access is unlimited, as shown in the bottom left photo. Install the tailpiece, drain body, and pop-up mechanism as well (as shown in the inset photo at left); see page 155 for more on installing a pop-up mechanism.

Install the sink.

Now you can lift the sink into position and slowly lower it onto the mounting bolts or bracket, as shown in the top right photo. Adjust the sink as needed from side to side.

Check the sink for level. Check to make sure the sink is level (lower right photo). Then fasten it to the wall with the screws or bolts provided, as shown in the top right inset photo.

Connect the supply lines. With the sink in place, you can connect the plumbing lines. Do the supply lines first, as the waste line would get in your way. Although flexible supply lines are easier to install, they're not very attractive. Since the supply lines are exposed on most wall-mount sinks, it's best to use chrome supply tubes. Thread the tubes through the mounting nuts, wrap a few turns of Teflon tape around the valve threads, and thread on and tighten the nuts. Trim these to length with a tubing cutter to fit into the shut-off valves. Wrap the threads of the shut-off valve with Teflon tape and thread on and tighten the nuts with an adjustable wrench. In our case, a cover conceals both the supply and waste lines. We used flexible supply lines to connect to the shut-off valves, as shown in the top photo.

Connect waste line and trap. For the waste line, adjust the trap and tailpiece to fit and tighten the slip nuts by hand, as shown in the middle left photo. Then, make a quarter-turn with slip-joint pliers. In many cases, you'll be connecting the new waste line to an existing line that has been cut off. Flexible rubber transition fittings are your best bet here. These have a hose clamp on each end; one is tightened around the new line, and the other is tightened around the existing waste line.

Add semi-pedestal and towel rack. The sink shown here has a couple of add-on parts that really dress it up: a semi-pedestal that covers the supply and waste lines, and a convenient built-in towel rack.

Drill mounting holes as needed for the semi-pedestal and attach it with the fasteners provided, as shown in the inset photo above. Then attach the towel rack, as shown in the bottom photo. The mounting screws for the towel rack are driven into rubber expansion plugs that fit in holes in the under-side of the sink.

A Raised-Height Toilet

TOOLS

- Adjustable wrench
- Slip-joint pliers
- Putty knife
- Caulking gun
- Screwdriver
- Socket set (optional)
- Hacksaw (optional)
- Tubing cutter (optional)

What's the big deal with a raised-height toilet? The unit is just a few inches taller than standard, but that can really increase ease and comfort. Basically, a higher seat means it's easier to sit on and rise from the toilet. (Consider also adding grab bars on one or both sides of the toilet as described on pages 164–165). If you are replacing a toilet, see pages 150–151 for detailed instructions on how to remove your old one. One thing to note about toilets: Older toilets often have much larger tanks and corresponding water capacity than new toilets—often up to 3 gallons versus 1.6 gallons. Many homeowners have been disappointed with the flushing performance of these low-capacity toilets. Some manufacturers, like American Standard, have responded by designing pressure-assist toilets. These use incoming water pressure to compress air in a special flush mechanism that creates greater flushing force.

Raised-height toilet anatomy. There are two main parts to a raised-height toilet: the tank and the bowl. The tank holds a preset amount of water to flush the existing contents of the bowl down the waste line (1.6 gallons in all toilets made after 1996, and up to 3 gallons in toilets made prior to 1996). When the flush handle is depressed, the lever arm raises a ball or flapper in the bottom of the tank—by way of either a chain or lift wires—so water in the tank can flow down

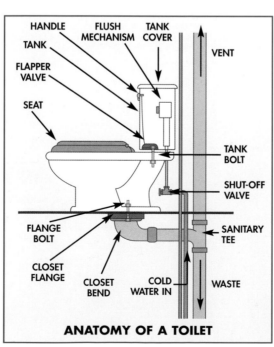

ANATOMY OF A TOILET

into the bowl. The water flows through a series of holes in the rim and with the aid of gravity, forces the contents of the bowl to exit through the integral trap, out through the horn, and down into the waste line via a sanitary tee.

After most of the water drains out of the tank, a flapper or ball will drop down to stop the flow. At the same time, the ballcock assembly inside the tank permits fresh water to flow into the tank, and into the bowl via the overflow tube. When a preset level (controlled by a float ball, a flow cup, or a metered valve) is reached, the water shuts off. If for any reason the ballcock fails to shut the water off, the water will rise above the overflow tube and drain down into the bowl. A wax ring fitted around the horn creates a seal between the toilet and the closet flange to prevent both water and sewer gas from leaking out. A spud gasket forms a seal between the tank and the bowl.

Prepare the closet flange. Regardless of whether you're replacing a toilet or installing a new one, you'll first need to prepare the closet flange to accept the bowl. This entails inserting closet flange bolts (sometimes referred to as "Johnny" bolts) into the slots in the closet flange. The T-shaped head is inserted into the larger opening on the flange and then slid around the curved slot to the correct position, as shown in the top photo. Bolts should be positioned on opposite sides of the flange so they're parallel to the wall behind the flange. These bolts pass up through holes in the bowl's base.

Create a seal. The most common way to create a seal between the bowl and the closet flange is to use a wax ring. There are two basic types of wax rings available: a simple ring of wax, and a ring with a rubber no-seep flange. The advantage that a no-seep flange has to offer is that the flange is added insurance against leaks. Alternatively, you can use a nifty "no-wax" ring (as shown here) manufactured by FluidMaster (www.fluidmaster.com). Instead of wax and its mess, these rings rely on foam rubber gaskets to create the seal, as shown in the middle photo. Note: This type of seal will require you to remove the rag from the closet flange now.

Install the bowl. With the seal in place, remove the rag in the closet flange used to keep out sewer gas (if it hasn't been removed previously), and position the bowl over the closet bolts. Gently lower the bowl in place (bottom left photo). Press firmly down on the bowl, but don't stand or jump on it: That would only over-compress the wax ring, resulting in a poor seal. Then thread the mounting nuts on the bolts and alternately tighten each nut until the bowl is flush with the floor (inset). Caution: Overtightening can and will crack the bowl base.

Install the tank. With the bowl in place, the next step is to attach the tank. Flip the tank upside down on the bowl and check to make sure the spud washer is in place. If it isn't, install it now. Now turn the tank over and set it on the bowl so the spud washer is centered on the inlet opening, as shown in the top photo. Then align the holes in the tank with the holes in the bowl and insert the tank bolts. To tighten the tank bolts, insert the tip of a long screwdriver in the slot in the bolt. Thread on the nut by hand until it's snug. Then switch over to a socket wrench or adjustable wrench to finish tightening. Proceed with caution, as overtightening can crack the tank. When done, place the cover on top of the tank.

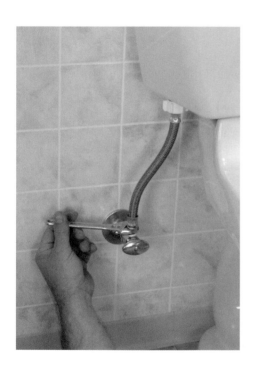

Connect to water supply. Now you can hook the tank up to the water supply. You can use flexible line for this (as shown in the middle photo), or install a chrome supply tube if the supply line is highly visible. Just make sure to wrap a few turns of Teflon tape around the threads of the shut-off valve before threading on and tightening the nut. On most toilets, the nut that secures the top of the supply line to the tank is plastic—tighten these by hand only, since pliers can crack them quite easily.

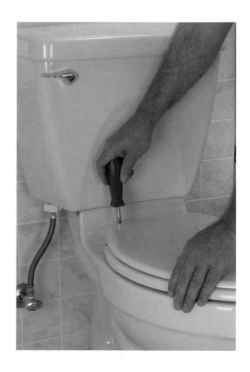

Finishing touches. All that's left is to add the seat (as shown in the bottom photo) and caulk around the base of the toilet. Not only does caulk provide added protection against leaks, but it also prevents water from seeping under the toilet when you mop the floor. A high-grade silicone caulk is best for this, as it will remain flexible over time, keeping the seal intact. Now you can turn on the water and test for leaks and proper flushing action.

Installing a Semi-Mount Sink

TOOLS

- Stud finder
- Tape measure
- Drill and bits
- Screwdriver
- Caulking gun
- Adjustable wrench
- Slip-joint pliers

A semi-mount sink like the one shown in the top photo is sort of a hybrid between a wall-mount sink and a drop-in sink. The sink fits in a recess in the countertop like a drop-in sink and provides the superior access of a wall-mount sink. But it doesn't mount to the wall—it attaches to the counter-top. As long as the countertop is fastened securely to the back wall and/or side walls, the sink will be solid. A semi-mount sink offers two other advantages over a wall-mount version: You gain countertop space, and the front of the counter conceals the plumbing below while still affording excellent access.

The sink shown here is made by American Standard, and requires that a countertop be built to house the sink. The company provides an accurate template that makes cutting the recess a breeze. Most kitchen and bath centers, along with home centers and specialty countertop shops, can make this simple countertop for you out of a variety of materials. We made the top shown here out of MDF (medium-density fiberboard) and covered it with

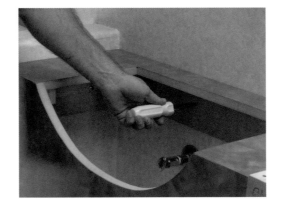

plastic laminate. As part of our master bathroom makeover (page 65), we added a short partition wall between the toilet and sink to support the end of the counter opposite the side wall. But this isn't absolutely neces-sary, as long as the countertop can be attached securely to the back wall and to at least one side wall.

Install the countertop. Locate the desired position of the countertop and fasten it the wall. Make sure your mounting screws hit the wall studs (middle photo).

Seal the countertop. Access to the back edge of the countertop is best now, so go ahead and apply a bead of silicone caulk to the back and side edges of the countertop where it butts up against the walls, as shown in the bottom photo.

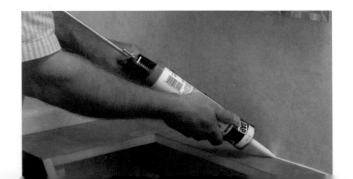

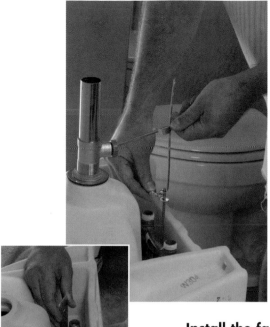

Install the sink. Now you can set the sink in the recess (top right photo) and secure it to the countertop with the fasteners provided. In many cases this will involve fastening a bracket to the underside of the countertop and then attaching the sink to the bracket. Finally, connect the supply lines to the faucet and trap to the waste line.

Install the faucet and pop-up mechanism. Now's also the best time to install a faucet, as shown in the top two left photos. See pages 154–155 for step-by-step directions on how to install a lever-style faucet.

Seal the sink. Before you install the sink in the countertop, apply a generous bead of silicone caulk around the edge of the cutout in the countertop, as shown in the bottom photo. This will create a watertight seal between the sink and counter.

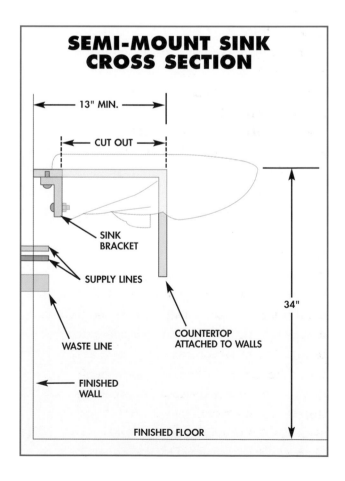

SEMI-MOUNT SINK CROSS SECTION

13" MIN.

CUT OUT

SINK BRACKET

SUPPLY LINES

WASTE LINE

COUNTERTOP ATTACHED TO WALLS

FINISHED WALL

34"

FINISHED FLOOR

Installing Grab Bars

TOOLS

- Tape measure and level
- Handsaw
- Drill and bits
- Hammer
- Screwdriver

Like so many aspects of an accessible home, grab bars are a boon to everyone. Even when strength or agility aren't issues, having something secure to hold onto for balance and stability is something we all appreciate. This is especially true in a bathroom, where using a toilet, shower, or tub can take effort—and where water can pose slippery hazards. Grab bars can be installed vertically or horizontally to provide the extra purchase we need to sit down or stand up; they frequently serve to help keep us steady when standing in front of a sink or mirror. For a grab bar to function safely, of course, it must be mounted securely; see the sidebar on the opposite page for mounting options.

All of the grab bars we used throughout our mature home makeover are manufactured by Safe-Access Systems Inc. (www.pba-na.com), the leading maker of anti-bacterial bathroom safety products and accessories. The company also offers coordinating shower seats, towel bars, and related items, all in several colors.

Install a wall cleat. Horizontal grab bars are typically installed 34" to 36" above the floor. The bottom of vertical grab bars generally starts around the same point. To install a horizontal grab bar, you'll need access to the wall studs. If you've gutted a bathroom as we did here, this is not an issue. Alternatively, you'll have to remove a section of the wall covering as needed. Cleats can be attached directly to the wall studs in cases where there's a space

between a tub or shower surround and the wall (as is the case here). Locate the cleat at the desired height and drive screws through it and into the wall studs, as shown in the top right photo. For a cleat to be flush with the wall studs, you'll need to install the cleat as if you were installing a wall-mount sink; see page 156 for more on this.

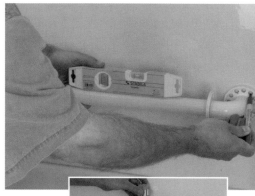

Locate the grab bar. With the cleat installed, you can cover it with drywall or the fixture—like the tub surround shown here. Measure up the desired distance (inset photo at right), and mark the locations of the mounting holes on the wall, as shown in the middle photo.

Drill mounting holes. Next, remove the grab bar and drill the recommended-size holes at each mounting-hole location, as shown in the bottom photo.

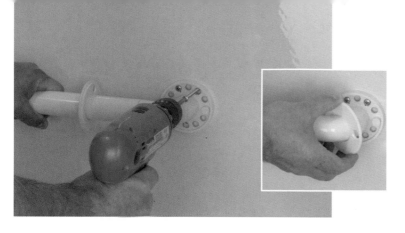

Install the grab bar. Install the grab bar by screwing it through the wall covering and into the cleat, as shown in the top photo; use the fasteners provided with the grab bar. On quality grab bars, these screws are concealed with a snap-on cover like the one shown in the inset photo.

GRAB BAR MOUNTING OPTIONS

■ There are three basic ways to install grab bars correctly: Have them attached directly to a fixture while they're still at the factory, attach them to a cleat or blocking fastened to the wall studs, or attach them to plywood sheathing fastened to the wall studs, as illustrated in the drawing below.

FACTORY-INSTALLED GRAB BAR

TUB OR SHOWER WALL

PLYWOOD REINFORCEMENTS MOLDED INTO UNIT OR ATTACHED WITH ADHESIVE

GRAB BAR

MOUNTING SCREW

SITE-INSTALLED WITH BLOCKING

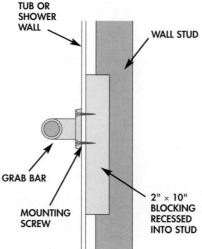

TUB OR SHOWER WALL

WALL STUD

GRAB BAR

MOUNTING SCREW

2" × 10" BLOCKING RECESSED INTO STUD

SITE-INSTALLED WITH PLYWOOD BACKING

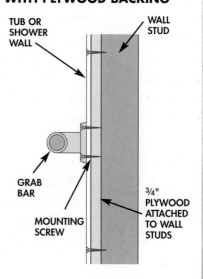

TUB OR SHOWER WALL

WALL STUD

GRAB BAR

MOUNTING SCREW

¾" PLYWOOD ATTACHED TO WALL STUDS

Factory-installed. Some mature-friendly tub and shower units can be ordered with the grab bars pre-installed—like the low-threshold Lasco Bathware shower we installed in the master bath makeover on page 65. The advantage to this is that the factory is better able to create a watertight seal; the downside is that since they're not attached to wall studs, the bars won't be as stout (but this is an issue only for large people).

Wall cleats. Wall cleats or blocking are the most common way to install a grab bar (as shown on the opposite page). A 2-by cleat is attached to wall studs, and the mounting screws of the grab bar are driven into the cleat.

Plywood sheathing. When a makeover for an accessible bathroom involves gutting a room, consider attaching a layer of ¾" plywood to the wall studs before installing drywall. Wrapping a bathroom in plywood like this allows you to mount a grab bar anywhere you want—without having to disturb the finished wall covering.

A Walk-In Bathtub

TOOLS

- Tape measure and level
- Screwdriver
- Socket set and/or adjustable wrench
- Caulking gun
- Drill and bits
- Slip-joint pliers
- Trowel (optional)

When climbing in and out of a bathtub is not an option, wouldn't it be wonderful to just open a door and walk in? It's possible, with the award-winning design from the folks at BathEase (www.bathease.com). There's no better time to install this unit than when the other fixtures have been removed and there are no obstructions. But, it's still not an easy project. The big challenge is about space and movement—moving the tub into an existing space. The problem is that most tubs fit into a recess with barely any clearance room. Trying to fit a new tub into this recess without damaging the existing walls is a very delicate, demanding process. So, it's always a good idea to get the tub in first before any finish wall work is done (like painting, wallboarding, or tiling). This way, if the walls do get dinged, they can be patched and then finished.

An acrylic or fiberglass tub is the easiest to install because it's much lighter than a cast-iron tub. Even acrylic tubs require two or three strong backs

to lift over any obstructions (such as piping sticking out of walls) and then place into position. The BathEase walk-in tub we used in our guest bathroom makeover (page 63) is made of slip-resistant acrylic, and uses NASA-recommended technology for its unique door gasket (seal). The first such tub in the market when it launched in 1988, the BathEase series now includes different models in a range of colors, all ADA-compliant.

Install the support cleats. The lips of most tubs are designed to sit on a set of cleats or stringers attached to the wall studs, as illustrated in the drawing below. Mark the recommended height of the cleats on the studs. Cut the cleats to length and attach them to the studs using a level to make sure they end up level, as shown in the top left photo on the opposite page. These cleats are

TUB/SHOWER FRAMING

CLEAT SUPPORTS RIM OF TUB/SHOWER

FLOOR MAY NEED EXTRA MORTAR BASE FOR SUPPORT

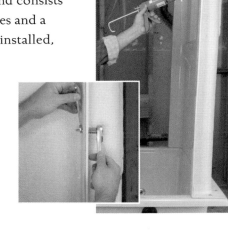

intended to level the tub, not support it fully. The bulk of the tub's weight should rest on the flooring. Also, for jetted tubs, you may need to frame an opening for a recess panel to provide access to the pump—this may not be necessary if the tub's apron (or portion of the apron) is removable.

heavy-duty fiberglass and consists of three pieces: two sides and a back. Before the tub is installed, you'll need to disassemble the surround (it bolts together), caulk all the joints with 100% silicone caulk, and reassemble it, as shown in the top right photos.

Install the drain and overflow. Create an opening for the drain/overflow in the floor, following the manufacturer's recommendations. Then install the drain/overflow onto the tub, as shown in the middle left photo. These are actually one of the most difficult fittings to install properly since they have many parts and fit onto the tub at an angle. Take your time with this and follow the installation instructions carefully. Odds are that you'll need to adjust parts a couple of times to get smooth operation of the drain plunger.

Attach the surround to the tub. Like BathEase, most bathtub manufacturers offer surrounds for their products. The BathEase unit comes bolted onto your tub at delivery when you order this option. The BathEase surround is molded from

Test the fit and secure the unit. To support the tub along its entire bottom, most manufacturers suggest setting the tub in mortar. If you're planning on this, now is the time to mix the mortar and apply it to the floor. If you choose not to use mortar, you'll need to support it with shims or with what most plumbers use now: non-expanding foam. Because this needs to be applied with the tub full, you'll have to wait to do this until the plumbing is hooked up (see page 168). With the help of a couple of strong backs, carefully lift the tub and set it in place onto the leveling cleats, as shown in the bottom right photo. Position it from side to side for

equal gaps on the ends, and allow the mortar to set overnight. Drill holes in the flange of the surround's perimeter every 8" to 10" and secure the flange to the studs with galvanized screws (inset photo above).

Connect plumbing and electrical. At what stage you hook up the plumbing and electrical will depend on your access. If there aren't any access panels, you'll have to do this before installing the tub, as described on page 167. Since we had gutted both the bathroom and the hallway for our makeovers, we had full access; so we installed the plumbing after the tub and surround were in place.

Have a licensed plumber install a diverter valve (bottom photo). If a shower is to be installed, copper tube will be run up the wall and terminate with a showerhead. Now is the time to support the bottom of the tub with non-expanding foam—make sure to fill the tub before applying this, and let it sit overnight before draining the tub.

A jetted tub (like the one we installed here) requires electricity to power the pump—usually a separate 15- to 20-amp line. To reduce the risk of shock, the power supplied to the pump must be protected by a GFCI (ground-fault circuit interrupter) breaker or receptacle. If you need to run a new line, you may want to consider hiring a licensed electrician. In most cases, the pump is wired with an electrical cord that can be plugged into the receptacle once it's in place.

Install the cover plates and handles. With the plumbing installed, you can add cover plates or escutcheons and faucet lever(s) and caps, as shown in the top right photo.

Install drywall. To complete the bathtub installation, apply drywall to the exposed studs. There's only one problem here—the flange of the tub surround. The drywall has to be installed over this and will go in at an angle. To prevent this,

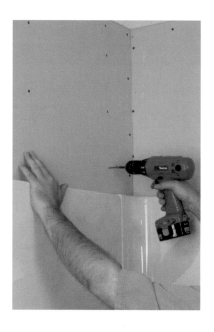

most pros will attach shims to the wall studs that are the same thickness as the flange. These can be cut from scraps of 2-by material, and go up quickly. With the shims in place, cut and install the drywall (see pages 120–121), and finish as desired. Finally, apply 100% silicone caulk around the perimeter of the tub and surround to create a watertight seal.

Installing a One-Piece Shower

TOOLS

- Handsaw or miter saw
- Hammer
- Tape measure and level
- Adjustable wrench
- Slip-joint pliers
- Drill and bits
- Caulking gun

For many mature folks, it's much easier (and safer) to take a shower than it is to wash up in a conventional bathtub. The major advantage of a shower unit over most bathtubs? The lower threshold of the shower pan is easier to get over than the rim of a bathtub (but not a walk-in tub like that shown on page 166). Unfortunately, the standard shower pan is still high enough to present an obstacle for many. That's why savvy fixture manufacturers like Lasco Bathware (www.lascobathware.com) have created low-threshold shower units like the one shown in the top photo and featured in our master bathroom makeover (page 65). What makes the Lasco unit especially mature-friendly is its built-in seat, grab bars, and adjustable handheld showerhead. This combination makes for a comfortable, safe, and enjoyable shower experience.

Most likely, you'll need to remove an existing tub or shower before installing the new unit; see pages 152–153 for detailed instructions on how to do this.

ONE-PIECE VERSUS MULTI-PIECE UNITS

■ The big thing to keep in mind when considering a one-piece vs. a multi-piece unit is that one-piece units are designed to be installed during new construction. The average one-piece shower unit will be too bulky to fit through most exterior doors, hallways, and bathroom doors. But none of these were impediments for our master bathroom because our home had a sliding patio door we could go through, wide hallways (thanks to our hallway makeover), and no narrow door openings, since we widened all our doors. With that said, we still had to remove the wall between the master bedroom and the bath, as shown in the photo at right, to be able to orient the unit and get it into the bathroom. Note also that we intentionally downsized the shower unit from 5 feet to 4 feet so we could fit it into the intended space—we used the narrow wall space left over to add built-in, open shelving (as described on pages 110–111).

3-PIECE   5-PIECE

Install the unit. With the plumbing in place, you can transfer the faucet locations onto the surround and drill the appropriate-sized holes. Be particularly exact in transferring these locations as there is little, if any, margin for error. Then insert the shower unit in the enclosure, as shown in the top right photo. A helper is extremely useful here: You'll probably need to lift the unit up and over the closet flange in the floor and navigate around any exposed supply and waste lines.

Build the frame. Most shower units come with explicit plans for the framing required to accept the unit. Consult these plans and cut and attach 2×4's as needed to create the frame, as shown in the top left photo.

Install the diverter. If you're installing a new shower faucet and diverter, now is the time to do it. Placement is fairly critical here, so if you're not comfortable with the job, hire a licensed plumber to install it, as shown in the bottom left photo. At the same time, you may or may not need to adjust the location of the waste line and trap.

Secure the unit. When it's in place, check the unit to make sure it's level and plumb, and then secure it to the surrounding wall studs. To do this, drill holes in the flange around the perimeter of the unit spaced 8" to 10" apart. Then secure the flange to the studs with galvanized screws or nails, as shown in the bottom right photo.

Add the drain. Once the unit is securely fastened to the wall studs, you can connect the drain to the waste line. In most cases, this means threading one half of a two-part drain assembly through the hole in the bottom of the shower pan and into the other half attached to the waste line, as shown in the top photo.

Install the cover plate and handle. Next, install the cover plates or escutcheons that cover the holes in the surround for the handle or handles, as shown in the middle left photo. Then add the handle or handles (inset photo) and secure them with the screw provided.

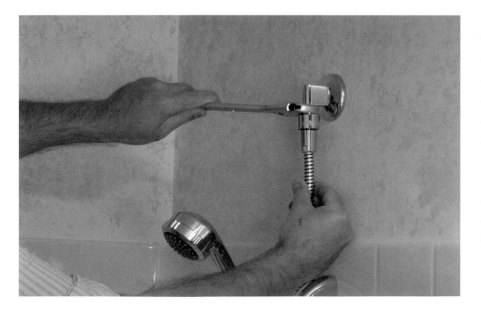

Install the showerhead. To compete the shower install, finish the walls and then attach the showerhead (or in our case, the handheld shower hose) to the showerhead pipe, as shown in the bottom photo. Finally, apply 100% silicone caulk around the perimeter of the shower unit to create a watertight seal, and install drywall as needed (pages 120–121).

A New Shower Door

TOOLS

- Hacksaw
- Electric drill and bits
- Tape measure and level
- Hammer
- Screwdriver
- Adjustable wrench
- Caulking gun

If you're tired of grappling with a shower curtain and would like to step up to a shower door, you'll find a wide variety of easy-to-install units available. Options include metal finish (chrome, brass, and brushed metal are common), along with type of glass: clear, opaque, and patterned. Additionally, you'll find units with one sliding door and one fixed, or both sliding. Our choice for this fairly compact bath was a sliding (bypass) unit from Lasco. In a roomier bath, you might want to choose one of their pivot (open-out) doors.

Although models vary, most sliding doors consist of six main parts: a top (or header) and bottom track (or sill), a pair of side channels (or jambs), and two doors, as illustrated in the drawing below. The doors are suspended from, and slide along, the top track which spans the jambs. The side channels fit into the bottom track and when caulked, create a watertight seal around the perimeter. Channels in the bottom track keep the doors from hitting each other as they're slid from side to side. One or more towel racks may attach to the doors.

Install the bottom track. Most sliding-door kits are designed to accommodate a range of showers and tubs—make sure to have your tub or shower measurements in hand when shopping for one. If necessary, the parts can be cut to length with a hacksaw. Follow the installation directions that come with your door. Most begin by having

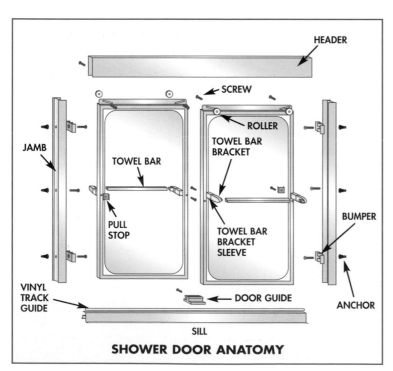

SHOWER DOOR ANATOMY

HEADER, SCREW, ROLLER, TOWEL BAR BRACKET, JAMB, TOWEL BAR, PULL STOP, TOWEL BAR BRACKET SLEEVE, BUMPER, ANCHOR, VINYL TRACK GUIDE, DOOR GUIDE, SILL

you install the bottom track. Measure and cut it to length if necessary (bottom right photo on opposite page); usually, it's cut narrower than the opening to allow the side

channels to slip over its ends. The bottom track is usually held in place with caulk. Apply beads of silicone as directed and set the bottom track in place. Some instructions will advise using masking or duct tape to hold the track in place until the silicone sets up.

Mount the side channels.

Since the side channels support the top track and the weight of the doors, it's important that they be firmly secured to the walls. In most situations they won't align with wall studs. That means you'll need to use wall anchors. Some door kits provide these, others don't. Use a level to plumb each side channel and mark the mounting holes onto the walls (middle left photo). Drill holes for your anchors and insert them in the wall. Reposition the side channel and secure with the screws provided, as shown in the bottom left photo.

Install the top track.

With the side channels in place, you can now attach the top track, cutting it if necessary to fit. Note: Since the top track usually fits over the side channels, it's cut longer than the bottom track. Set the track in place over the side channels and secure to the side channels if screws are provided for this, as shown in the top right photo. On some door kits, the weight of the doors is all that's required to hold the top track in place.

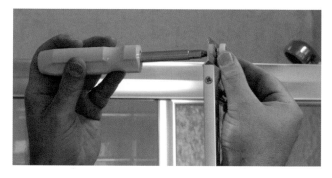

Hang the doors. Now you can install the doors. You most likely will first have to attach the rollers to the top flanges of each door, as shown in the middle right photo. Take care to follow the directions, as the rollers are often installed differently on each door. When the rollers are in place, grip a door firmly on the sides with both hands and lift it up into a channel in the top track so the rollers slip into place. Then pivot the door in so the bottom rests in the corresponding channel in the bottom track. Repeat for the other door. If towel bars are supplied, attach them now (bottom right photo) and then apply caulk around the inside and outside perimeters, as directed.

9

ELECTRICAL

Electricity powers our lives, and its energy has nothing to do with age or ability. How we use that energy, though, can be readily adapted to suit a mature life stage. Each of the projects described in this chapter, ranging from simple to complex, offers better access, convenience, and safety over existing fixtures.

We'll show you how to replace hard-to-operate electrical switches with mature-friendly paddle switches, and how to install under-cabinet lighting so you can see what you're cutting on a kitchen countertop. Then we'll step up to more advanced projects like installing recessed lighting, a remote-controlled ceiling fan, and a built-in wall heater. Kitchen improvements like installing a wall oven and a cooktop finish out the chapter, along with how to install a fan/light in the bathroom that senses humidity and motion...and even operates the controls for you automatically.

Paddle Switches

TOOLS

- Screwdriver
- Electrician's pliers (optional)

Upgrading an electrical switch from the standard small toggle to the mature-friendly paddle-style switch (like the one shown in the top photo) is an easy job with immediate rewards. Instantly, the switch will be easier to turn on and off for everyone in the home. Many switch manufacturers offer paddle-style switches in a variety of wiring options and colors. Two- and three-way switches are common, and some are available with built-in illumination to make them super-easy to find in the dark.

Install the new switch. The new paddle switch can now be installed. Basically you'll reverse the steps taken to remove the old switch. Connect the wires to the new switch, and tighten the screws (as shown in the photo below). Press the new switch and wiring carefully into the electrical box and secure the switch to the box (inset below). Install a new cover plate, restore power, and test.

Remove the old switch. To upgrade to a paddle-style switch, first turn off the power to the switch at the fuse or breaker panel. Then take off the cover plate by removing the two mounting screws. Next, remove the screws that secure the switch to the electrical box and gently pull the switch out of the box. If needed, make a wiring diagram to make reconnection easier. Loosen the wiring screws, as shown in the bottom left photo, and lift the wires off the screws.

Under-Cabinet Lighting

TOOLS

- Screwdriver
- Awl
- Electric drill and bits
- Hammer (optional)

Cabinets installed over a countertop, as most are, tend to block light. This can be a real problem—especially in a mature home, since the countertop is where most food prep is done. You can illuminate, that is, eliminate this dangerous situation, by installing under-cabinet lighting like that shown in the top photo. Although you can mount an under-cabinet light anywhere under the cabinet, most makers recommend locating the light as close to the cabinet front as possible for the best coverage.

Install the puck. When you've determined the best position for the light, locate and mark the holes for the mounting hardware. Many lighting manufacturers provide a template for this. Position the template where you want the light. Then, using an awl, press through the template at the hole locations to make depressions on the underside of the cabinet. Alternatively, hold the light in position and mark the mounting hole locations on the underside of the cabinet with an awl. Next, use the recommended-size bit to drill pilot holes for the screws (provided with most lights). Drive the screws through the lamp and into the bottom of the cabinet (bottom left photo). Then snap on the diffuser (bottom left inset photo).

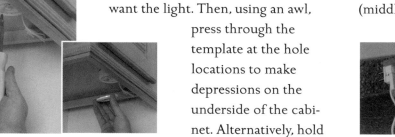

Connect the wiring. Strip-style under-cabinet fixtures are designed to plug into a wall receptacle. Halogen fixtures typically require adding a low-voltage transformer that plugs into a standard receptacle. The transformer is pre-wired: All you need to do is fit the connector on the end of the puck into the connector on the wiring (middle right photo). Route the wires to the receptacle using the wire clips provided. Then attach the two-part plug to the end of the wire (inset photo); attach the two-part on/off switch to the wiring, plug it in, and test.

HALOGEN PUCK KITS

■ Some areas in the kitchen may not need an entire strip of lights. Here's where small, individual "puck"-shaped halogen lights are ideal. Puck lights are available in packs of two or more and can be mounted exactly where you need the light and then wired together. Wiring is simple: The wiring just snaps into each light. The final puck in the string is connected to a low-voltage transformer, which is plugged into a nearby receptacle.

Installing Recessed Lighting

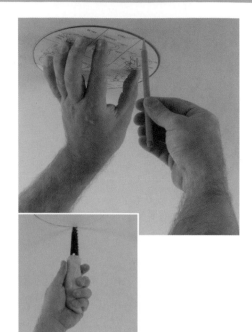

Recessed lights are a plus for any home: They're easy to install, they direct light exactly where you need it and, because they're recessed into the ceiling, they make the ceilings look higher. They are also so unobtrusive that they won't clash or interfere with other design elements in the room. Recessed lights are designed to be mounted in one of three situations: in suspended ceilings, in new construction, and—the one that applies most to makeovers—in remodel work. Recessed lights are either single units or two-piece units consisting of a mounting frame and a light; see the bottom right drawing.

Cut an opening in the ceiling. The first step in installing a recessed light is to identify where you want the light. Then locate the ceiling joists with a stud finder. If you have easy access to the ceiling from above, you can secure the fixture to the joists. When access is restricted, you'll use the remodel clips provided with the light. If possible, locate the light between joists to provide plenty of clearance during installation. Mark the hole for the light on the ceiling either using the template provided (top right photo), or with a compass set to the recommended radius. Then use a drywall saw or a reciprocating saw to cut the opening for the light, as shown in the inset photo above.

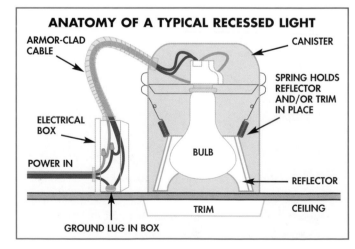

ANATOMY OF A TYPICAL RECESSED LIGHT

ARMOR-CLAD CABLE

CANISTER

SPRING HOLDS REFLECTOR AND/OR TRIM IN PLACE

ELECTRICAL BOX

BULB

POWER IN

REFLECTOR

GROUND LUG IN BOX

TRIM

CEILING

Connect the wiring. Now you can run power to the light; the simplest way to do this is to route the power cable of the old overhead light to the new location. This way the existing light switch can control the lights. If this isn't possible, run new lines or have them installed by an electrician. Note: If your ceiling is insulated, as most are, make sure you buy lights that are rated to come in contact with insulation. When you've got the power cable routed to the light, follow the manufacturer's directions to wire the fixture (make sure the power is off).

Insert the can in ceiling opening. With the fixture wired, the next step is to insert it through the hole and up into the ceiling, as shown in the middle left photo. Clear out any insulation to make room for the fixture. If your light is a two-piece model, separate the parts as directed and drop the can through the frame. Then push the frame through the hole in the ceiling and attach it to the ceiling with the remodel clips provided.

Lock the can in place. How you secure the light to the ceiling will depend on whether the light is a single or two-piece unit. For single units, like the one shown in the middle left photo, this is simply a matter of forcing the attached spring clips up into the can so

the clips pivot out over the ceiling to pull the lip of the fixture firmly into the ceiling. You can push the clips into place by hand (top right photo), with needlenose pliers, or with a screwdriver.

On two-piece units, the light typically attaches to the mounting frame via a set of screws. You'll need either a "stubby" screwdriver or a small socket wrench to tighten these, as space inside the can is cramped.

Add trim and bulb. On some recessed lights, the bulb holder may need to be threaded into a socket up inside the light. If the light you are installing is like this, install the bulb holder now. Now you can add the decorative trim. There are many different ways trim is held in place. On some models, the trim is simply pushed up into the fixture and spring clips hold it in place, as shown in the middle right photo. Other lights use long springs that must be hooked onto tabs up inside the fixture to secure the trim. After you've added the trim, screw in the recommended light-bulb (inset photo at right), restore power, and test.

Built-In Wall Heater

TOOLS

- Stud finder
- Tape measure
- Drywall saw
- Electrician's pliers
- Screwdriver

As we age, our body's thermostat often gets a bit wacky. We tend to be cold more frequently and this is an issue especially in the bathroom, when disrobing or drying off. Wouldn't it be nice if you could just warm up the room without turning up the heat to the entire house? You can—with the assistance of a wall-mounted heater like the one shown in the top photo. The unit shown here is made by Broan-Nutone (www.broan.com) and is just one of many types and sizes they offer. The heater is designed to fit between existing wall studs, as illustrated in the drawing below. This is great for do-it-yourselfers, because no re-framing is necessary.

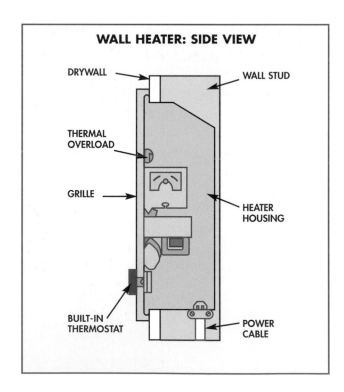

WALL HEATER: SIDE VIEW

- DRYWALL
- WALL STUD
- THERMAL OVERLOAD
- GRILLE
- HEATER HOUSING
- BUILT-IN THERMOSTAT
- POWER CABLE

Cut an opening in the wall. To install a "between-the-studs" heater like the one shown here, start by locating the wall studs with a stud finder. Then measure up the recommended distance from the floor and lay out the opening. Cut the opening with a drywall saw, as shown in the bottom photo. For the bathroom shown here, we replaced an old, narrow heater with a new wider, more efficient unit.

Secure the housing in the opening. Remove the heater from the housing and route the power cable through the punchout hole in the housing. Then push the housing into the opening and secure

it to one or both wall studs, as shown in the top left photo. Note: If you're not replacing a wall heater, you'll need to run a dedicated power line to the bathroom; consult a licensed electrician if needed.

Install the heater. With the wiring complete, the heater unit can now be installed in the housing. To do this, insert the unit into the housing, taking care not to pinch any wiring. When it's in place, secure it to the housing with the screws provided, as shown in the top right photo.

Add the trim. All that's left is to add the trim or cover to the heater, as shown in the bottom right photo. Restore power to the heater and test. Note that most new heater units will smell a bit when first turned on as the various coatings on parts are heated up for the first time.

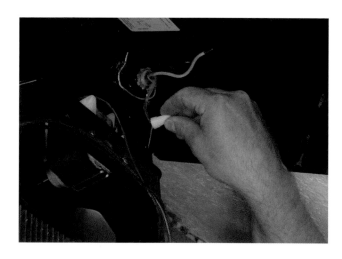

Connect the wiring. Following the manufacturer's wiring diagram, connect the heater to the electrical cable, as shown in the middle photo. Make sure to ground the line as directed by the manufacturer. For the heater shown here, this means attaching the ground wire to a clip attached to the housing, as shown in the bottom left photo.

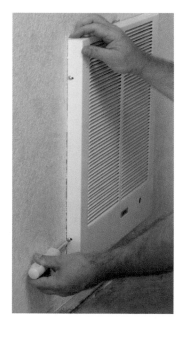

Home Heartbeat Awareness System

Did I unplug the coffeepot? Is the garage door closed? We all sometimes slip up on these everyday issues, and now there's a "home awareness" system that can help assure safety, security, and peace of mind. Called "Home Heartbeat," this wireless, plug-and-use system lets you monitor and receive updates on a wide range of home devices and systems. You can use it in your own place, or let it help you stay in touch with what's going on at another residence.

Developed by the Eaton Corp. (www.eaton.com), the system uses sensors to monitor for problems like water leaks and flooding. It also gives updates on home appliances, the status of doors and windows, routine maintenance schedules—it can even oversee the comings and goings of family members. The system sends emails or text messages to cell phones when a problem is detected.

While the product is very high-tech, you don't need to be an engineer to install and use it. As the company says, "If you can plug in a lamp, use a remote control, and apply stickers," you can use Home Heartbeat.

HOME HEARTBEAT KIT COMPONENTS

■ The Home Heartbeat Starter Pack includes the basic items needed to monitor a home away from home: a base station, home key, open/closed sensor, power adapter, and telephone jack cord. The system can be expanded to add up to 30 additional sensors, and is customizable to suit individual needs.

Base station. This central unit collects information from various sensors, then relays it to either the HomeKey (a small alerting device), a cell phone, or email.

Attention sensor. Touch-activated, this unit works as an instant messenger when a family member needs help, or wants you to know they got home safely.

Open/closed sensor. Tiny peel-and-stick sensors affix to windows and doors and report status to an alerting device, cell phone, or email.

Power sensor. From cooktops to computers, if it plugs into a wall socket, this sensor will let you know if something was left on.

Water sensor. In a basement or laundry room, this device reports on flooding, or a burst pipe, before it gets out of hand.

Video/Security System

You don't need an elaborate alarm system to feel more secure at home. Today's options include new door-answering systems that not only let you see who's there before you answer, but also let you talk with your visitor. The Video Door Answering Systems from NuTone (www.nutone.com) come in two versions: one basic, one with added features.

The basic system includes a camera, a 4" color monitor that lets you see who's at the door, a door chime, and hands-free door communications. You can touch a button (or pick up the phone-like, optional handset) and talk with your visitor—or not, as you choose. A more deluxe version offers a 7-inch, drop-down monitor that fits under kitchen cabinets, and can be used to view TV or listen to the radio, a speakerphone, and an optional second camera for the back door. Both systems are compact and simple to use.

VIDEO SYSTEM COMPONENTS

■ NuTone's Video Door Answering Systems come in two versions: Both let you see and talk with visitors before you open the door, using small video cameras and quality sound transmission. The more elaborate model has an optional second camera, and lets you use the monitor to watch TV or listen to music.

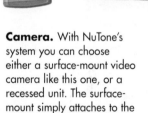

Camera. With NuTone's system you can choose either a surface-mount video camera like this one, or a recessed unit. The surface-mount simply attaches to the wall next to the door frame.

Drop-down monitor. This larger color monitor fits under kitchen cabinets to let you see visitors, watch TV, or listen to music.

Installing a Ceiling Fan

To increase home comfort while saving on energy costs, a quality ceiling fan is a smart addition to any room. Not only does it add a touch of style, but it also offers cooling in the summer and heating in the winter. In the summer, of course, a fan can help circulate air-conditioned air or even cut down the need for extra chilling. In the winter, a ceiling fan set on low in the downdraft mode can actually help drive warm air from near the ceiling down into the living space. We chose a low-profile, whisper-quiet Hunter Fan for our living room/dining area. It's virtually wobble-free and installs in a snap. No tools are needed for either the blades, which snap securely into place, or the glass light shades: One twist does it. And, the blades are reversible: Ours are maple on one side, darker cherry on the other. Finally, a remote control makes operation more convenient for anyone.

There are three ways to mount most fans: flush, standard, and angled. The type you choose will depend on the height and slope of your ceiling. The general rule of thumb is that you need at least 7 feet of clearance between the fan blades and the floor. Also, because ceiling fans are heavy, they must be installed in electrical boxes especially designed to handle this weight or be attached to heavy-duty boxes that are affixed directly to your ceiling joist.

Attach the mounting plate. To install a ceiling fan, start by turning off the power and threading the electrical wires coming out of the box  through the opening in the ceiling plate. Then, using the hardware provided, secure the ceiling plate to the electrical box and/or ceiling joist as shown in the top right photo.

Hook the fan onto the mounting plate. Because ceiling fans tend to be heavy, most fan manufacturers have added a hook on the ceiling plate to suspend the fan while you connect the wires. If your ceiling plate has one of these, hook the fan onto it, as shown in the bottom photo. If it doesn't, enlist the aid of a helper to hold the fan while you connect the wires.

Connect the wiring. Wiring for most ceiling fans is pretty straightforward; consult the manufacturer's wiring diagram for your fan. Connect black to black and white to white. Connect the ground wire to the ground wire of the fan or to the grounding lug on the ceiling plate. Most fans come with wire nuts for making these connections.

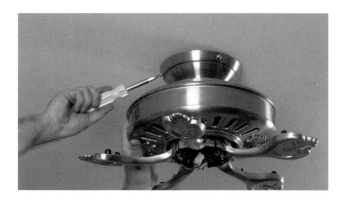

Attach the fan to the mounting plate. With the wiring complete, stuff the wires up through the opening in the ceiling plate and into the electrical box. Now you can attach the fan to the ceiling plate. Unhook it and position it on the plate so the holes in the fan align with those in the ceiling plate. Secure it with the screws provided, as shown in the middle photo. Here, the weight of the fan can make this difficult. Consider getting a helper to hold and align the fan while you drive in the mounting screws. Also, most fans have a canopy that slips over the fan housing to conceal the inner workings and keep out dust. If your fan has a canopy like the one shown here, slip it in place and secure it with the screws provided.

Install the blades and diffusers. All that's left is to add the blades and light shades. Mounting systems differ from screw-on to snap-in. Some fans instruct you to attach the blade brackets to the fan before mounting it to the ceiling; others don't. If you haven't attached the blade brackets to the fan, do so now. Then attach the blades with the hardware provided. On the Hunter Fan shown here, no hardware is required for this; you simply position the blade on the bracket and lock it in place with the built-in locking lever, as shown in the top right photo. Hunter has even made installing the light shades hardware-free; you just insert the shade in the lamp bracket and twist to

lock it in place (bottom photo). Turn the power back on and test the fan. If the fan wobbles, use the blade-balancing kit provided with the fan.

Installing a Wall Oven

TOOLS

- Screwdriver
- Diagonal cutters and wire stripper
- Driver/drill and bits
- Saber saw (optional)

Wall ovens are just plain wonderful, whether your back is 18, 80, or in between, whether you're standing or sitting. Unlike a traditional range oven, a wall oven doesn't make you bend down to see if the casserole is done, or reach and strain to lift out a roast. You can buy these back savers as single ovens, double ovens, or in combination with microwave ovens, like the high-performance KitchenAid appliances we used here. The state-of-the-art microwave pairs with a convection oven for both access and superior results.

Prepare the opening. Wall ovens are becoming so popular that most cabinet manufacturers now offer tall cabinets specifically designed to house wall ovens. The only problem is, they're designed to fit a wide variety of ovens. This means you'll likely need to modify the opening to fit your oven. Consult your oven's installation manual for the required opening. Lay out the opening on the cabinet front and cut

the opening with a saber saw, as shown in the bottom left photo. (Note that we covered the base of the saw with tape to prevent it from scratching the cabinet face.) You'll also need a suitable electrical receptacle to plug it in behind the oven, and a gas line if it heats with gas. Running electrical and gas lines is best left to professionals.

Slide in the unit.

With the opening cut to size, and power (and gas if necessary) run to the oven, you can slide the unit into the cabinet. Hook up the oven and then slide it in place, as shown in the middle photo. Many of these units are surprisingly heavy, so it's best to enlist the aid of a helper to lift the unit into place.

Secure unit and add trim. Many wall ovens are secured to the cabinet by driving screws through flanges on the sides of the oven and into the face of the cabinet, as shown in the photo at left. With the oven secure, add the trim provided to conceal the mounting screws, as shown in the right photo.

A New Cooktop

TOOLS

• Screwdriver

Stand-alone cooktops are steadily growing in popularity, partly because they're especially well suited for installation in today's popular islands and peninsulas. We installed this KitchenAid model in our accessible kitchen because it features up-front controls that don't make you reach over a heated surface to operate, whether you're sitting or standing. Its flat, ceramic top is easy to clean, and you can adapt the cabinetry below for roll-up access (see page 97 for more on this). The use of the space below the cooktop will depend on the type of venting chosen. For overhead range hoods (as shown here), this area now becomes always-desirable storage. If a downdraft vent system is used, the space is likely to be taken up with the vent unit or remote blower.

As with a wall oven, you'll need a suitable electrical receptacle to plug in the cooktop, and a gas line if it heats with gas. Running electrical and gas lines are best left to professionals.

Prepare the opening. Whichever type of venting is used, installing the actual cooktop is quite simple. All you need to do is use the manufacturer's template to mark the location of the opening for the cooktop on the countertop, and cut it out. For a solid-surface countertop (like the one shown here), the opening will need to be cut by the fabricator. Openings on solid-surface countertops should also be protected against heat damage by applying a layer of metallic tape to the edges, as shown in the bottom left photo, to help dissipate heat.

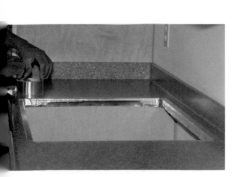

Attach the mounting clips. Most cooktops attach to the countertop with some type of special mounting hardware. The KitchenAid cooktop shown here uses brackets attached to the bottom of the cooktop (middle photo).

Slide in the cooktop and secure it. With the mounting hardware in place, insert the cooktop in the opening, as shown in the bottom right photo. Then thread the screws provided into the brackets you installed on the cooktop. Drive the screws up until they butt up against the underside of the countertop, as shown in the inset photo. Tighten the screws to pull the cooktop down tight into the countertop.

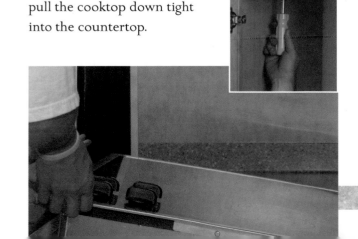

Installing a Motion-Activated Fan/Light

TOOLS

• Stud finder (optional)
• Drywall saw
• Screwdriver

Every bathroom needs ventilation to remove moisture-laden air. Otherwise, mold and mildew will grow and spread. For both our bath upgrades, we turned to Broan (www.broan.com) for a combination fan/light unit that automatically turns itself on and off.

Exhaust fans for bathrooms less than 100 square feet should remove air at the rate of 1 cubic foot per minute (CFM) per square foot. For example, the typical 5' × 7' bathroom has 35 square feet, so it requires a fan rated at 35 CFM or higher. For bathrooms larger than 100 square feet, fans are keyed to the type and number of fixtures in the bathroom. Fixtures are rated as follows: toilet (50 CFM), shower (50 CFM), tub (50 CFM), jetted tub (100 CFM). So, a bathroom with a jetted tub, toilet, and separate shower should use a 200-CFM fan. Note: Enclosed toilets should have their own fan.

To prevent mold and mildew, a timed switch is an excellent feature. Combined with the safety aspect of its automatic light, our Broan model is a perfect fit for aging in place. It features a SmartSense fan/light designed to sense changes in room humidity and to automatically activate the fan until humidity levels reach normal. The unit is also designed to sense the movement of occupants in the room and to automatically activate the light or night light. The sensor unit continuously monitors the area and operates the light until no further motion is detected.

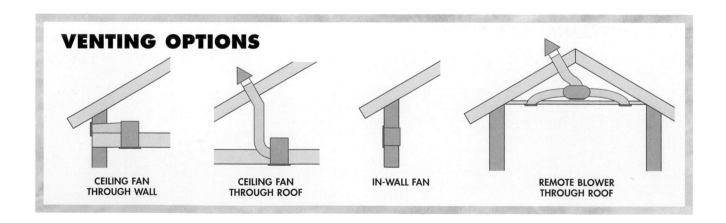

VENTING OPTIONS

CEILING FAN THROUGH WALL

CEILING FAN THROUGH ROOF

IN-WALL FAN

REMOTE BLOWER THROUGH ROOF

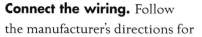

Cut an opening in the ceiling. Because they're heavy, ceiling vents need to be attached to, or supported by, the ceiling joists. If you're replacing an existing fan as part of your makeover (as we did here), remove the old fan and increase the opening as needed (top left photos). For new fans, locate the joists with a stud finder and lay out the opening on the ceiling, using either the fan itself or a pattern, if provided. If you're replacing a fan, pull the existing vent hose through the opening and attach it to the fan or the duct connector. New fans will need ducting to be installed (see the sidebar on the opposite page for ducting options). Flexible hose is by far the easiest to run. Just make sure to angle the hose down about 1/4" per foot toward the vent cap so moisture trapped in the hose will run out to the exterior instead of back down into the fan.

Route the wiring and insert the housing. Route the new or existing wiring through the punch-out hole in the fan housing and secure it to a cable clamp (photo at left). Then insert the housing into the opening (as shown in the top right photo), and press the housing in so it's flush with the ceiling. Secure it either to brackets that run between the joists, or to the joist, with screws.

Connect the wiring. Follow the manufacturer's directions for

wiring the fan. Some units can be fairly complex: Besides the fan motor, they may have a light and a night light. Connect the fan wiring to the existing or new wiring with wire nuts, as shown in the inset photo.

Install the fan and trim. With the fan's wiring complete, insert the fan into the housing, as shown in the photo at right. Secure it and plug the wiring harness into the appropriate connector. If your fan has additional electronics (like the sensing board described in the sidebar below), adjust and install it now. Then all that's left is to install a bulb (if it's a combination fan/light) and the diffuser, or light shade (photo at right).

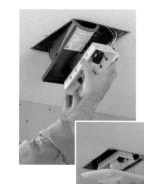

ADJUSTABLE SENSORS

■ Both humidity- and motion-sensing controls on the Broan fan/light can be adjusted as follows:

Humidity: You can adjust the humidity sensor control to keep the fan turned on for 5 to 20 minutes after humidity levels have returned to normal.

Motion: When mounted on an 8' ceiling, the motion sensor views an elliptical pattern roughly 10'× 15'. Adjustments can be made to the viewing area by blocking portions of the sensor lens with the adhesive film provided with the fan.

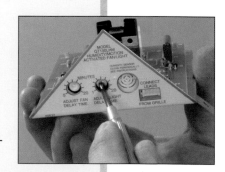

Index

METRIC EQUIVALENCY CHART

Inches to millimeters and centimeters

inches	mm	cm	inches	cm	inches	cm
1/8	3	0.3	9	22.9	30	76.2
1/4	6	0.6	10	25.4	31	78.7
3/8	10	1.0	11	27.9	32	81.3
1/2	13	1.3	12	30.5	33	83.8
5/8	16	1.6	13	33.0	34	86.4
3/4	19	1.9	14	35.6	35	88.9
7/8	22	2.2	15	38.1	36	91.4
1	25	2.5	16	40.6	37	94.0
1 1/4	32	3.2	17	43.2	38	96.5
1 1/2	38	3.8	18	45.7	39	99.1
1 3/4	44	4.4	19	48.3	40	101.6
2	51	5.1	20	50.8	41	104.1
2 1/2	64	6.4	21	53.3	42	106.7
3	76	7.6	22	55.9	43	109.2
3 1/2	89	8.9	23	58.4	44	111.8
4	102	10.2	24	61.0	45	114.3
4 1/2	114	11.4	25	63.5	46	116.8
5	127	12.7	26	66.0	47	119.4
6	152	15.2	27	68.6	48	121.9
7	178	17.8	28	71.1	49	124.5
8	203	20.3	29	73.7	50	127.0

mm = millimeters   cm = centimeters

Photo credits

Alcoa (www.alcoa.com): page 26 (middle).

American Standard (www.americanstandard.com): page 33 (middle), page 47 (right).

Amerock (www.amerockhardware.com): page 37 (top).

Anso (www.anso.com): page 22 (bottom), page 32 (top, bottom right), page 48 (top right)

Armstrong (www.armstrong.com): page 32 (bottom left), page 174, page 174.

Bach Faucet (www.bachfaucet.com): page 146.

Bosch Appliances (www.boschappliances.com): page 1, page 12 (middle), page 48 (top left).

Broan-NuTone (www.broan.com): page 183 (all).

Cooper Lighting (www.cooperlighting.com): page 50 (middle), page 51 (top left).

Crossville (www.crossvilleinc.com): page 12 (top), page 19 (bottom), page 20 (top), page 89 (top), page 112.

Daltile (www.daltile.com): page 44 (top).

Delta (www.deltafaucets.com): page 41 (top), page 44 (middle).

DPI (www.decpanels.com): page 49 (left top and bottom).

DuPont Corian (www.corian.com): page 14 and 40 (bottom).

Duro-Med (www.wdrake.com): page 101 (bottom).

Eldorado Stone (www.eldoradostone.com): page 26 (top and bottom), page 28.

Formica (www.formica.com): page 36 (top).

FSC (www.fschumacher.com): page 21, page 23 (middle), page 49 (top right).

Hansgrohe (www.hansgrohe-usa.com): page 45 (top).

Home Heartbeat (www.homeheartbeat.com): page 182.

Hy-Lite (www.hy-lite.com): page 30 (middle).

Jeld-Wen (www.jeld-wen.com): page 22 (top left), page 27.

Kitchenaid (www.kitchenaid.com): page 12 (bottom), page 23 (top), page 42 (top right and bottom), pages 42–43 (bottom), page 43 (top left and right).

Kohler (www.kohler.com): page 19 (top), page 49 (bottom right), page 50 (top right).

KraftMaid (www.kraftmaid.com): page 36 (middle).

Lasco (www.lascobathware.com): page 5, page 16 (bottom), page 45 (middle), page 46 (top).

LiteTouch (www.litetouch.com): page 31 (top right).

LG Hi-Macs (www.lghi-macs.com): page 6, page 90.

Marvin Windows (www.marvin.com): page 30 (top).

Merillat (www.merillat.com): page 2.

Miele (www.miele.com): page 15 (bottom), page 33 (bottom), page 42 (top left).

Mohawk Industries (www.mohawkind.com): page 15 (top), page 20 (middle and bottom), page 36 (bottom).

North Coast Medical (www.beabletodo.com): page 101 (top and middle).

ODL (www.odl.com): page 11, page 30 (bottom).

Pella Windows (www.pella.com): page 48 (middle, bottom left, and bottom).

Porter-Cable (www.portercable.com): page 121 (bottom).

Price Pfister (www.pricepfister.com): page 41 (bottom).

Progress Lighting (www.progresslighting.com): page 31 (bottom), page 51 (top right).

Rev-A-Shelf (www.rev-a-shelf.com): page 37 (bottom left).

Safe Access (www.pba-na.com): page 46 (all bottom).

Staron (www.getstaron.com): pages 32–33 (top), page 40 (top and middle), page 41 (middle), page 44 (bottom).

Tessera (www.chicagofaucets.com): page 16 (middle), page 47 (left), page 59.

Thermador (www.thermador.com): page 31 (middle).

Timberlake Cabinet Company (www.timberlake.com): page 8, page 14 (top), page 23 (bottom), page 38 (bottom), pages 38–39 (top).

Velux (www.velux..com): pages 10–11, page 22 (top).

Verilux (www.verilux.net): page 50 (both bottom).

Vetter Windows (www.vetterwindows.com): page 31 (top left).

Vitraform (www.vitraform.com): page 34.

Wellborn Cabinet, Inc. (www.wellborn.com): page 13, page 37 (both far right), page 39 (all bottom).

Whirlpool (www.whirlpool.com): page 43 (bottom right).

Wilsonart (www.wilsonart.com): page 128.